THE 2015 PRO FOOTBALL BEAST BOOK

The 2015 Pro Football Beast Book

©2015 Killer Tribes
PO Box 1, Intercourse, PA 17534

Written by Bryan Allain | @bryanallain | @profootballbeast
BryanAllain.com | ProFootballBeast.com

ISBN: 978-0-9883729-4-8

THE 2015 PRO FOOTBALL BEAST BOOK

The Definitive (and Slightly Ridiculous) Guide to Enjoying the 2015 Pro Football Season

Bryan Allain

The 2015 Pro Football Beast Book

TABLE OF CONTENTS

—

How To Use This Book   7

PART I
1 Thing The Seahawks Should Have...   13
On The Changing Of The Extra Point   14
199 Words On Flat Balls   16
25 Things J.J. Watt Did This Summer   17
19 Fantasy Draft Thoughts   19
48 Fantasy Team Names You Can Use...   22
One More Section   23

PART II
Team Previews For All 32 Teams   26 - 89

PART III
Weekly Viewing Guides   92 - 125

PART IV
Your Post-Season Predictions   128
My Post-Season Predictions   129
Weekly Knockout/Suicide Pool Tracker   130
Grocery Lists   133
Championship Game Kickstarter Predictions   137

PART V
Thank Yous and What Not   4 8 15 16 23 42

The 2015 Pro Football Beast Book

HOW TO USE THIS BOOK

aka, The Introduction

—

I mean, you know how to use a book at this point in your life, but just a few thoughts before you start flipping pages like a maniac.

PART I - Consider this your appetizer (think calamari or spinach dip, not mozzarella sticks). My take on a few of the hot topics of the NFL like whether or not Tom Brady's balls matter, how J.J. Watt spent his off-season, and if moving the extra point back was a terrible idea (spoiler alert, it was). Feel free to read at your leisure.

PART II - I wrote season previews for all 32 clubs, but I know you'll probably flip to your favorite team first and that's cool. After that, you might read about everyone else in the division, and by that point I hope you realize, "Hey, these are fun!" and you read them all. If your reaction is more along the lines of, "Hey, these team previews suck and make me want to punch baby monkeys!" then I am sorry for making you angry. Also, please don't hurt the baby monkeys.

I'd love to think that this section will be something you can quickly flip to at any point during the season to glance at upcoming schedules, names of coaches, and to see how incredibly wrong I was when I wrote these up.

On each team page there's a spot where I put in my prediction and a spot for you to do the same. Go through all 32 teams and guess their record and we'll see which one of us had more right come January 2016.

PART III - If the Beast Book was only season previews, it would be hard to justify keeping it around all season long. You'd probably throw it on a bookshelf or use it to start a fire since no one has old newspapers laying around anymore. That was not the fate I wanted for this book, so I put in the weekly viewing guide.

Every week you see the schedule of games, including kickoff times and which network is carrying it. Now, maybe you don't care about which network carries a football game, but I do, so I put it in. That's the beauty of writing your own book.

If you're a degenerate gambler like myself (not really), you can use the schedule to record betting lines, which team you chose, and whether the home, road, favorite, or underdog covered the spread. I only expect 2% of you to do this, but I'm like low fat milk; I'm all about the 2%. And terrible dairy jokes.

There are also three uniquely interactive elements I put on each weekly spread to make the football season a more fun and communal experience:

Fantasy Trash Talk Mad Libs are a fun way to creatively talk smack with the idiots you play with in your fantasy league. You can be as nasty or silly as you want, and all you need to do once you fill it out is snap a picture, share it on social media, and tag them so they see it. I can't wait to see how creative you get with this.

Each week you'll find a new Prop Game that you can share in a similar fashion to Mad Libs, only instead of trying to humiliate someone, the goal is to win prizes. If you can nail all 10 questions, you may win a prize that week. 7 or more right and you'll earn an entry into the year-end grand prize drawing.

There are some official rules for when you need to post your entry by, where you need to post it, and how to officially submit your entry for consideration if it's a winner. You can get all those here:

ProFootballBeast.com/weeklygame/.

The final element on the weekly pages is your Power Poll Rankings. The goal here is to try and look smart. At any point during the week (or during the games on Sunday), let us know who you think the Top 5 and Bottom 5 teams in the league are. Each week also features an extra question like "Top 3 Most Overrated Holidays" or "Top 3 MVP Candidates Right Now" just to keep it light. These will be an easy way to get discussion going on your social media accounts, and they'll also be fun thing to look back on later in the year to see just how wrong we all were.

PART IV - Everything that didn't fit into the first three parts of the book goes here, including my post-season predictions, a place for you to make your post-season predictions, a suicide pool tracker that helps you see which teams you have yet to choose, a grocery list for when you need to look like you're doing more than watching football, and so on.

Well, there you have it.

My goal for the Beast Book was to create the book that I wish I had in my hands every time I sat down to watch football. I wanted something that would put the info I need at my fingertips, would help me keep track of the things I wanted to keep track of, and would make watching football an even more enjoyable experience.

So, that's what I did.

I hope you enjoy it too.

Bryan Allain
July 29, 2015

The 2015 Pro Football Beast Book

PART I*

RANDOM THOUGHTS, LISTS AND ESSAYS

*The part before all the other parts**

(it comes before Part II)*

***no other part comes before this part. If parts were children in a family, this would be the oldest child who has more responsibility than the other kids but also had stricter rules because his parents were just figuring things out and yet, they still did an amazing job and gave me a great childhood and I love you mom and dad.

1 THING THE SEAHAWKS SHOULD HAVE DONE DIFFERENTLY LAST SEASON

aka, oops.

—

Gave the ball to Marshawn.

ON THE CHANGING OF THE EXTRA POINT

aka, why this rule will probably change again next year

In case you missed it, the extra point has changed.

It used to be that a team set up at the 2-yard line following a touchdown to try for an 18-yard kick (worth one point) or a conversion across the goal line (worth two).

This spring, the owners voted to change that. Now, if a team wants their single digit, they have to move back to the 15-yard line for a 32-yard kick. And if they want to go for two, the ball is placed on the 2-yard line. (A third option is that they can pretend they are kicking from the 15-yard line, and instead try to score two from there, but probably only Andy Reid will try that.)

Pretty small change, right? Wrong. THIS IS A TERRIBLE IDEA. Let me explain.

First off, we need to look at why the owners are doing this. This change happened because the extra point kick was made 96% of the time. It's a boring, predictable play. And because two-point conversion attempts are far less boring, the owners moved the kick back in hopes that more teams will opt for the more exciting play.

Problem is, they won't.

Based on field goal stats from the same length, we know the new extra point is going to be converted somewhere between 90-94%. While slightly more risky than the old extra point, it is still a much safer play than the 50/50 odds you get with a 2-pt conversion.

I'm telling you right now, 32 out of 32 coaches would rather blame their kicker for missing a chip shot kick than take the blame themselves because they went for two. There may be a couple more 2-pt tries over the course of a year, but on the whole, coaches are still going to go for the 1-pt kick attempt, just like they always have.

So it's a wash right? Wrong.

The unintended consequence of this change is that it has put more emphasis on kickers determining the outcome of football games. Does anyone, other than the kickers and their moms, actually want that?

How are you going to feel in December when your team rallies from down two touchdowns in the 4th quarter, only to lose the game by a point because your kicker missed a 33-yard kick worth one point? Spoiler alert: not happy.

What should they have done instead?

Some have suggested that coupling this rule tweak with moving the 2-point try to the 1-yard line (instead of the 2-yard line) would have made this rule change more robust. Their thinking is that it would have increased the odds of successfully converting the 2-pointer, compelling more coaches to try it.

While I agree with the logic, I still think most coaches would opt for the kick until the game situation gave them no other choice.

And when you get down to it, this is the problem with the rule change. It happened because owners wanted to rid the game of a play that worked 96% of the time.

Was it boring? Yes.

Was that okay? Yes.

No one wanted more intrigue with the extra point kick because no one wanted more football games being decided by something that used to be an afterthought.

If the owners wanted to reduce the number of extra point kicks from the game, they should have gotten rid of it altogether. They didn't, and all you can do at this point is hope it's not YOUR kicker that sends an extra point try wide right to keep you out of the playoffs in December.

This rule change is up...and it's no good.

249 WORDS ON FLAT BALLS

aka, an open letter to Tom Brady

—

Tom,

We know you like the footballs flat. You should have said so from Day One.

You should have told us, "I like my footballs right at the minimum, maybe even a little lower. Some guys like them above the limit, I go the other way. It's not a big deal."

But it seemed like you were lying, and the public loves outing liars, so it became a big deal. It should not have been a big deal. (If anyone reading this disagrees, tell me how upset you were about Aaron Rodgers admitting during a televised game that he liked footballs that were illegally over-inflated. Didn't care much about that, did you? Exactly.)

Unless it comes out that the NFL was lying and manipulating this story, you'll never be able to outrun it, Tom, but that's okay. We like our heroes (and villains) flawed anyway.

Your statistics speak for themselves. You are one of the best ever. You may have known your balls were too flat, and you may have lied about it, but it's all good. You'll do your time. And maybe I'm going out on a limb here, but I'm pretty sure you're going to crush it in 2015, flinging around 13-psi footballs for 12 (or 16) games.

Love the Uggs, tell Gisele we said hi, and one time my grandma said I looked like you.

Bryan

PS...this letter was written on July 2, 2015. If Tommy didn't lie, I take it all back.

25 THINGS JJ WATT DID THIS SUMMER

aka, I know watt you did last summer
—

J.J. Watt had a monster 2014.

How monster? How about 20.5 sacks, 4 forced fumbles, 1 fumble return TD, 1 interception return TD, 1 safety, and 3 receptions for 3 touchdowns. Oh, and don't forget one of the most memorable mic'd up segments ever against the Titans in Week 13.

How do you top that? You ramp up the intensity over the off-season and come into camp ready to raise your game to a new level. And from what we've heard on the rumor mill, J.J. Watt did exactly that.

According to our sources, here's what J.J. Watt did this summer:

1. He drank 5 gallons of milk from the teat of an angry cow every morning.

2. He took down an enemy helicopter with a slingshot and a marble while interning with Seal Team 6.

3. He dated the entire roster of Houston Texan Cheerleaders in the month of June.

4. Every one of those cheerleaders proposed to him.

5. He learned the craft of glass-blowing in between bench-press sets. (He was benching 830 lbs.)

6. He ate an air conditioner.

7. He showed Elon Musk a few fatal design flaws with the Hyperloop Transport System that had gone unnoticed by his team of engineers and scientists.

8. He provided the last piece of critical evidence needed to indict FIFA officials.

9. He rewrote the Maze Runner trilogy on yellow legal pads and made it twice as good.

10. He carded hole-in-ones at the 12th at Augusta, the 17th at Sawgrass, and the par-5 14th at St. Andrews.

11. He climbed Mt. Everest with his shoes tied together while carrying a wounded goat.

12. He hacked Priceline into paying him money to stay at 5-star hotels.

13. He outran the Higgs-Boson particle.

14. He wore a burmese python as a belt at the request of the python.

15. He knew the python wanted to be his belt because he learned parseltongue and was able to communicate with it.

16. He captured and jailed forty drug lords while on vacation in Mexico.

17. He slept eight hours combined the entire summer.

18. He mapped his own genetic code and found a cure for brain freezes in the process.

19. He built a better mousetrap that not only catches rodents, but turns their feces into aspirin and releases them back into to the world as productive members of society.

20. He invented a new leg muscle group.

21. He saved 16% on his car insurance in 14 seconds.

22. He built a fire without oxygen, heat, or fuel.

23. He wrote, produced, and directed Taylor Swift's *Bad Blood* video.

24. He developed a devastating new spin move in the mirror that his reflection couldn't even keep up with.

25. He convinced himself he was terrible last year and that he still has something to prove. Opposing offensive lineman...you've been warned.

19 FANTASY DRAFT THOUGHTS

aka, how to crush one of the best days of your entire year

—

Lest you think I'm trying to push myself as a fantasy expert, I'm not.

Last year I was in five leagues, and I only one won. The year before, I was in six leagues. SIX LEAGUES! And I went 1 for 6. (And yes, the 2013 and 2014 wins were in the same league. In fact, the only reason I wrote this book was to let the world know I'm the 2-time defending champion of the Amish Bouvas League! It's in print, suckers!!!)

So when it comes to fantasy I'm just like you…I usually lose. But I have been in enough leagues over the years to learn a few things, so take note and see if any of these tips can help you improve on your fantasy experience.

1. If you really want to win your league, start preparing a few weeks before your draft. It doesn't have to become a full-time job, just find a little time each day to read the NFL headlines and find one or two fantasy podcasts to listen to in the car. In a few episodes you'll learn about five guys to avoid and five guys to target that will make you smarter than half the guys in your league. That might be all it takes.

2. If that sounds like a waste of time and you only have an hour to prepare, print out a cheat sheet ahead of time, put an 'x' next to guys you'd rather not draft, and put a star next to guys you like. Then, when you are on the clock, don't be afraid to reach for your "starred" guys. Cheat sheets are great, but they are not gospel.

3. If you only have twenty minutes to prepare for your draft, who are you, Bill Gates? Geesh, find some time for some hobbies in your life.

4. If you only have ten minutes to prepare for your draft, do not play fantasy football.

5. If you're in any type of keeper league, bring everything you need from last year. Draft results, final standings, whatever. I've been in leagues where guys were 100% sure they knew who they couldn't keep based on last year's draft, and they were 100% wrong. Thankfully I had done the research and brought the documentation to prove it. Sure, that guy hated me and wanted to drown me in the buffalo chicken cheese dip (what a way to go), but in the end we kept everything on the up and up.

6. If you crap your pants at your draft you have two options: a) Immediately change your team name to reflect what just happened (The Pants Crappers, The Accident, The Browns, etc.) or b) Finish drafting, give your team to someone else, and find a new league. I recommend (b), unless you're the type of person who enjoys hearing about how you crapped your pants every August for the rest of your life.

7. If you're live-drafting in a room with people (vs. online), bring a list of NFL players who dropped out of the league 5-10 years ago. Nothing gets a few laughs in the room quite like shouting out one of those names when another owner is taking too long to make a pick. Start with 'Fred Taylor!' or 'Deuce McAllister!' and go from there.

8. It's great to be the guy who knows the most in the room, but its not always great when everyone else knows that too. When someone says, "Who does Mike Wallace play for now?" don't immediately bark out, "the Vikings!" Let someone else answer it. And if no one else knows, you can casually say, "I think Minnesota?" as if you're not sure. In fantasy, just like in real life, no one likes a know-it-all.

9. On a related note, don't correct people for mispronouncing names unless you know the room really well. By all means, though, make fun of them in your head for thinking it's "Joy-qua Bell" or "Lattaviss Murray".

10. Everyone and their mom is going to want Odell Beckham Jr. on their team this year because of that catch and how fun it is to root for him (not to mention how uncoverable he looked last year). If you really want him, be prepared to take him a round before you should. And if someone else grabs him first, don't whine about it like everyone else will. Cross him off your list and act like a professional!

11. The only thing worse than taking a kicker in the 8th round because the guy before you just took the first kicker is being the guy who says, "Uh oh, a run on kickers!" Don't be that guy.

12. Also, don't take a kicker in the 8th round.

13. And don't take a defense in the 8th round either. You're so much better off using those mid-round picks on hit-or-miss RBs or WRs than on a defense. You'll get a defense later, and they will be fine. It's not going to lose you your league. But getting lucky with Jeremy Hill in the 11th round last year? That might have won it for you.

14. Speaking of which, do you know who the top five defenses were in most leagues last year? Philly, Houston, Buffalo, St. Louis, and Green Bay. That' right, Seattle was sixth, and some doofus took them instead of drafting a solid third wide receiver.

15. The first time you try to take someone who has already been drafted, we will kindly let you know. The second time, we will yell at you. The third time, it's a pick axe to the base of your skull. Pay attention.

16. Don't be afraid to draft guys who are suspended for a few games or out with injuries for the first month of the season. These guys will always go a few picks later than they would have otherwise, but when they're starting for you in your fantasy playoffs, you'll be happy they were on your bench during September.

17. If you want a rule changed in your league, don't wait until Round 10 of your draft to start complaining about it. Bring it up a week before the draft, and if it seems like you might get some traction with it, bring it up again before you start drafting.

18. Give yourself about three to five "nice pick!" compliments to throw out during the draft. It makes you seem like a nice person (even if you're not), and it lightens the mood in the room. Don't go much higher than five, though, or you look like an idiot who thinks every football player is a future Hall of Famer. That's Jon Gruden's corner.

19. If you're in a league with me, disregard everything I just said.

48 FANTASY TEAM NAMES YOU CAN USE IF YOU WANT

aka, because if your team name sucks, you've already lost

—

- Jeff Fisher Stache Lice
- Your Worst Nightmare
- Ed Hochuli For President
- The Shirtless Harbaughs
- Bring Back the Horse Collar
- My Bench > Your Starters
- The George Selvie Sticks
- The Ineligible Retrievers
- Aaron Donald Trump
- Facemasking the Kicker
- The Girly Gurlies
- The Groin Encroachment
- Go Lick a Plunger
- Radio Shack Stock
- Your Face Scares Me
- Gronk Make Touchdown
- Rear Naked Bootleg
- I Believe Brian Williams
- Unsportsmanlike Con Duck
- Shady McCoy Party
- In Memory of Cecil the Lion
- Frosting the Kicker
- The Two-Minute Drill Bits
- Jay Cutler is Striking
- Delay of Shame
- Shark Week Every Week
- The Wheel Routes
- The Dress was White and Gold
- The Pick Sixes
- Zoos Aren't Fun
- Fifth and Goal
- Unnecessary Smoothness
- Bob Kraft's White Collars
- FIFA Was Framed
- Take Me to Barry Church
- Scrubbing Bubble Screens
- Noah's Ark's Bathroom
- Belicheck Seems Fun
- Flat Balls, Furry Uggs
- The Dez Bryant Tape
- Johnny Tebow
- 50 Shades of Dominance
- The Amish Light Bulbs
- The Best Team in This League
- The Wilfork Diet
- Andrew Luck Falsetto
- Twerking the Kicker
- I'll Pick a Name Later

ONE MORE SECTION

aka, something smart or funny

—

This is just a filler paragraph to take up space for the sake of formatting, and I will replace this text over the next few days and weeks and months so that it is smart and funny and makes people laugh and think about life and football and chicken wings and really I don't know what else to say so I will hit the return key after this period.

But I need a few more lines of filler text, so let's keep going and see what happens. Maybe it would be funny if I left one of these filler paragraphs in the final edition of the book? Probably not, but if you are reading this right now, then I did.

And the thing is, you HAVE to be reading this right now because if you weren't reading this, you wouldn't be reading this. So clearly I HAVE put this paragraph into the final edition of this book.

Just by typing these words I have altered the future and created a parallel universe and because of that I am a genius and should be celebrated with a statue in front of every museum and every football stadium and every house in America. Okay I think that's enough filler for now. Don't forget to replace all of these later, you moron.

PART II*
TEAM PREVIEWS

*The second part**

(it comes between parts I and III)*

***technically, there are a lot of parts that could come between I and III if we were dealing with all rational numbers. It could be Part 1.4 or Part 1.93631, so just saying it comes between Parts I and III might not be specific enough. On the other hand, when working with Roman Numerals there is only one thing that comes between I and III, so maybe this is all a moot point and you should have spent this time on a different page of this book or working in your yard. My apologies.

DALLAS COWBOYS

'14: 12-4 | 1st NFC East | #3 NFC Seed

WK 1	NYG	2015 SCHED	
WK 2	@phi	WK 10	@tb
WK 3	ATL	WK 11	@mia
WK 4	@no	WK 12	CAR
WK 5	NE	WK 13	@was
WK 6	BYE	WK 14	@gb
WK 7	@nyg	WK 15	NYJ
WK 8	SEA	WK 16	@buf
WK 9	PHI	WK 17	WAS

Claim to Fame: For the first time in 3 years 'dem Cowboys DID NOT finish 8-8.

Team Anagram to represent last season:
Classy Wood Lab

LOOKING AHEAD TO 2015...

Key Additions: Darren McFadden (OAK), Greg Hardy (CAR), Jasper Brinkley (MIN), Byron Jones (draft)
Key Subtractions: DeMarco Murray (PHL), Bruce Carter (TB), Dwayne Harris (NYG), George Selvie (NYG), Jermey Parnell (JAX), Justin Durant (ATL), Anthony Spencer (NO)
Key Multiplication: 4 x 3 = 12
Key Division: 39% of their locker room use shampoo first when in the shower, the other 61% use soap first (and think the shampoo-first people are insane).

(HC) Jason Garrett, 6th yr | **(DC)** Rod Marinelli, 2nd yr | **(OC)** Scott Linehan, 2nd yr
Base Defense: 4-3

EVERYTHING ELSE YOU NEED TO KNOW...

Do they play in London this year?
Nope. (They beat JAX in London, 31-17, in 2014.)

Do they play in Cairo this year?
Nope. The NFL does not play games there, you moron.

How many prime time games are they scheduled for?
Five, but their biggest game, hosting the champs in Week 5, is an afternoon kickoff.

Do you have any other thoughts on their schedule?
Based on last year's records it's the 9th easiest in the league...two division games to open the season means they need to come out swinging...but, being done with the Eagles and Giants by November 10th sets up a fairly easy second half of their schedule as they only play one team that finished with a winning record last year after Week 9...Washington will likely be trying to play the spoiler role in Week 17, lucky for Dallas, they suck.

EVERYTHING ELSE YOU NEED TO KNOW (CONT'D)...

What is their best-case and worst-case scenario for the season?
Best case, they go 16-0 and win the Super Bowl. Worst case, Jerry Jones has one more facial reconstruction surgery that turns his face into a super black hole that sucks in the entire universe, ending life as we know it.

Can we play a fantasy football version of two lies and a truth?
Sure. One of these points might help you win your fantasy league, two definitely won't.

1. Tony Romo averaged 2.8 sideline snot rockets per game last year, 10th among NFL QB's in 2014. If your league counts snot rockets as a category, that's gross.

2. Dez Bryant played all of 2014 with eleven broken ribs, a fractured ankle, and no cartilage in his entire body. Now healthy, look for a slight boost in his numbers.

3. Cole Beasley was targeted seven or more times in three of his last seven games in 2014 (playoffs included). With Witten getting older, Beasley could see an increase in targets in 2015 and might be a good late-round flier?

Is there anything about this team I don't know that I probably should?
The Cowboys team physician, Dan Cooper, is not respected in the locker room because he refers to Tylenol and Advil as "little teeny-weeny booboo pills."

Enough nonsense, what's your prediction for this season?
Jerry Jones believes his offensive line could get Betty White to rush for 1000 yards, but I'm not sure his running back-by-committee approach is going to work, especially if McFadden and his papier-mâché body get injured early. Speaking of backs, no team's fortunes rely as heavily on one spine as the Cowboys' do with Tony Romo. If he stays healthy, I think the division is theirs to lose, especially now that the Dez Bryant is signed. The upgrade from Monte Kiffin to Rod Marinelli at D.C. was huge last year, and it's the reason they should, at the very least, be able to maintain defensive mediocrity in 2015. If you're looking for a bright spot on defense, it could be their front seven. Greg Hardy returns from suspension just in time to face the champs, Sean Lee is back from injury, and Demarcus Lawrence and Tyrone Crawford look like budding stars on the defensive line. If the Cowboys start 4-4 I think their easy second-half schedule puts them in position to finish strong, win the East, and make it back to the post-season.

The Pro Football Beast Prediction: **10-6**

Your Genius Prediction: _____ <--- Go ahead, grab a pen and write it here.

PHILADELPHIA EAGLES

'14: 10-6 | 2nd NFC East | Missed Playoffs

WK 1	@atl	2015 SCHED	
WK 2	DAL	WK 10	MIA
WK 3	@nyj	WK 11	TB
WK 4	@was	WK 12	@det
WK 5	NO	WK 13	@ne
WK 6	NYG	WK 14	BUF
WK 7	@car	WK 15	ARI
WK 8	BYE	WK 16	WAS
WK 9	@dal	WK 17	@nyg

Claim to Fame: No offense ran more plays per game in the NFL last year (70.4).

Team Anagram to represent last season:
Pillaged Pee, Hail, Ash

LOOKING AHEAD TO 2015...

Key Additions: DeMarco Murray (DAL), Byron Maxwell (SEA), Sam Bradford (STL), Kiko Alonso (BUF), Walter Thurmond (SEA), Ryan Mathews (SD), Tim Tebow (ESPN), Nelson Agholor (draft)
Key Subtractions: LeSean McCoy (BUF), Nick Foles (STL), Jeremy Maclin (KC), Nate Allen (OAK), Bradley Fletcher (NE), Brandon Boykin (PIT)
Key Multiplication: 5 x 3 = 15
Key Division: 39% of surveyed Eagles' fans think Chip Kelly is a genius, 61% smashed an ice ball into the survey taker's face because he wasn't wearing an Eagles jersey.

(HC) Chip Kelly, 3rd yr | **(DC)** Billy Davis, 3rd yr | **(OC)** Pat Shurmur, 3rd yr
Base Defense: 3-4

EVERYTHING ELSE YOU NEED TO KNOW...

Do they play in London this year?
Nope. Never have, either.

Do they play in Rio De Janiero this year?
Nope. The NFL does not play games there, you doofus.

How many prime time games are they scheduled for?
Five, including the Monday Night Football opener in Atlanta.

Do you have any other thoughts on their schedule?
Based on last year's records it's the 10th easiest in the league...they play on Thanksgiving for the second year in a row (@ DET)...three of their four December opponents finished 2014 with a winning record...their last five games are outdoors in potentially cold weather...both Dallas games are in the first half of their season.

EVERYTHING ELSE YOU NEED TO KNOW (CONT'D)...

What is their best-case and worst-case scenario for the season?
Best case, they go 16-0 and win the Super Bowl. Worst case, Chip Kelly goes on a season-long trading binge, completely switching out his roster six times by Thanksgiving. He eventually admits to hating football but loving roster moves, and tries to trade the entire Philly fan base to Atlanta. Their fans start World War III, ending life as we know it.

Can we play a fantasy football version of two lies and a truth?
Sure. One of these points might help you win your fantasy league, two definitely won't.

1. Don't worry about Ryan Mathews stealing fantasy points from DeMarco Murray this season because Murray plans to saw Mathews in half on the eve of their season opener.

2. I'm not saying it's going to happen, but I've got a hunch that Donovan McNabb might be suiting up for the Eagles at some point this year. Nothing wrong with spending your last pick on him, just in case. (Let the other owners laugh, what do they know anyway?)

3. TE Zach Ertz split time with Brent Celek in 2014 because of Celek's prowess as a run blocker, yet still had a career-high 58 catches. This offseason Ertz hired an offensive line coach to improve his blocking game, so look for more snaps and more catches in 2015.

Is there anything about this team I don't know that I probably should?
Chip Kelly averaged 3.1 TKW* in '14. While that was good enough to lead the NFL, it doesn't come close to Andy Reid's 27.4 TKW in '09. (*TKW = Tastykakes eaten per week)

Enough nonsense, what's your prediction for this season?
It fascinates me that Chip Kelly borrowed from the offense to improve the defense, but I get it. This defense was 31st in yards per completion last year, and with opposing receivers like Dez and OBJ on the schedule twice, it's understandable why they overhauled their secondary. Plenty of questions remain - can Brandon Graham fill Trent Cole's shoes, for example - but it's a step in the right direction. Is Sam Bradford the long-term answer for the offense? I don't know and neither do you. His ability to stay healthy is the great unknown. DeMarco Murray will miss that O-line in Dallas, but he'll still produce as long as he stays on the field. An easy schedule early will help with the learning curve, but I think this team is still a year away from winning the division. Unless, of course, they start TEBOW!!!

The Pro Football Beast Prediction: **9-7**

Your Genius Prediction: _____

NEW YORK GIANTS

'14: 6-10 | 3rd NFC East | Missed Playoffs

WK 1	@dal	2015 SCHED	
WK 2	ATL	WK 10	NE
WK 3	WAS	WK 11	BYE
WK 4	@buf	WK 12	@was
WK 5	SF	WK 13	NYJ
WK 6	@phi	WK 14	@mia
WK 7	DAL	WK 15	CAR
WK 8	@no	WK 16	@min
WK 9	@tb	WK 17	PHL

Claim to Fame: Allowed 4.9 yards per rush last year, the worst in their franchise's history.

Team Anagram to represent last season: Yawning Stroke

LOOKING AHEAD TO 2015...

Key Additions: Shane Vereen (NE), George Selvie (DAL), Dwayne Harris (DAL), Ereck Flowers (draft)
Key Subtractions: Antrel Rolle (CHI), Stevie Brown (HOU), Walter Thurmond (PHL)
Key Multiplication: 4 x 1 = 4
Key Division: 39% of Eli Manning's thoughts are football-related, 61% focus on the nuances and subtleties of toothpaste commercials.

(HC) Tom Coughlin, 12th yr | **(DC)** Steve Spagnuolo, 1st yr | **(OC)** Ben McAdoo, 2nd yr
Base Defense: 4-3

EVERYTHING ELSE YOU NEED TO KNOW...

Do they play in London this year?
Nope. They won the first ever London game, 13-10, over the Dolphins in 2007.

Do they play in Amsterdam this year?
Nope. The NFL does not play games there, you idiot.

How many prime time games are they scheduled for?
Five, including four in the first six weeks.

Do you have any other thoughts on their schedule?
Based on last year's records it's the 12th easiest in the league...they caught some nice climate-related breaks traveling to Buffalo in early October and to Miami in December instead of the other way around...three of their four games against 2014 playoff teams are at home...their only home game in November is hosting the Patriots.

EVERYTHING ELSE YOU NEED TO KNOW (CONT'D)...

What is their best-case and worst-case scenario for the season?
Best case, they go 16-0 and win the Super Bowl. Worst case, Odell Beckham Jr. leaves the NFL during the pre-season to pursue a career in the circus and the Giants replace him with a juggling bear. With nothing to look forward to, and a premonition that the bear will not be good at football, their fans start World War III, ending life as we know it.

Can we play a fantasy football version of two lies and a truth?
Sure. One of these points might help you win your fantasy league, two definitely won't.

1. Tom Coughlin is considering suiting up at RB for the Giants this year as a player/coach. Avoid taking anyone in the Giants backfield, as he could vulture touchdowns and yards as a significant ground game threat, despite being more brittle than burnt bacon.

2. With President Obama signing into law a bill that requires all fantasy leagues to award 20 points for every one-handed catch made in warm-ups this year, Odell Beckham Jr. will obliterate every scoring record ever. If you don't have the 1st pick, quit your league.

3. If you're the last team to take a QB in a league with 12 or more teams, don't sleep on Eli Manning as a viable option. His 63% completion percentage and 14 INTs were career-bests in 2014, and that was without Victor Cruz for most of the year.

Is there anything about this team I don't know that I probably should?
The team style guide lists their official shade of red as "Tom Coughlin's angry face during a December night game after an Eli Manning pick six." Very specific.

Enough nonsense, what's your prediction for this season?
I had the G-men penciled in for a return above the .500 mark this year until they lost LT Will Beatty to a pectoral injury. The unsettled O-line hurts what surely would have been a more productive offense, considering Eli conquered the learning curve for Ben McAdoo's scheme last year. What he needs is protection, because the weapons are in place; Victor Cruz is back from knee surgery and Shane Vereen will have a big role in this offense. On defense, questions abound. Can Landon Collins replace Antrel Rolle? Will JPP return to play this year after his explosive Fourth of July? Can Steve Spagnuolo return as the D.C. with the same fire he brought seven years ago? It's improve or "adios" for Coughlin, but I think he does just enough to stick around.

The Pro Football Beast Prediction: **8-8**

Your Genius Prediction: _____

WASHINGTON REDSKINS

'14: 4-12 | 4th NFC East | Missed Playoffs

WK 1	MIA	2015 SCHED	
WK 2	STL	WK 10	NO
WK 3	@nyg	WK 11	@car
WK 4	PHL	WK 12	NYG
WK 5	@atl	WK 13	DAL
WK 6	@nyj	WK 14	@chi
WK 7	TB	WK 15	BUF
WK 8	BYE	WK 16	@phi
WK 9	@ne	WK 17	@dal

Claim to Fame: Had the worst point differential (-137) in the NFC last year.

Team Anagram to represent last season:
Wins Shrink Goats Den

LOOKING AHEAD TO 2015...

Key Additions: Terrance Knighton (DEN), Stephen Paea (CHI), Chris Culliver (SF), Dashon Goldson (TB), Brandon Scherff (draft)
Key Subtractions: Brian Orakpo (TEN), Chris Chester (ATL), Ryan Clark (retired)
Key Multiplication: $2 \times 2 = 4$
Key Division: 39% of Daniel Snyder's money is more money than you have, 61% is way way way way way way way more money than you have.

(HC) Jay Gruden, 2nd yr | **(DC)** Joe Barry, 1st yr | **(OC)** Sean McVay, 2nd yr
Base Defense: 3-4

EVERYTHING ELSE YOU NEED TO KNOW...

Do they play in London this year?
Nope. Never have, either.

Do they play in Dublin this year?
Nope. The NFL does not play games there, you imbecile.

How many prime time games are they scheduled for?
Three, all against division opponents.

Do you have any other thoughts on their schedule?
Based on last year's records it's the 13th easiest in the league...three of their first four are at home, including opening the season hosting the Dolphins and Rams...they have no division games from Week 5 through Week 11...they finish with two divisional road games, not that it should matter at that point anyway.

EVERYTHING ELSE YOU NEED TO KNOW (CONT'D)...

What is their best-case and worst-case scenario for the season?
Best case, they go 16-0 and win the Super Bowl. Worst case, Daniel Snyder refuses to change the team name, Jay Gruden refuses to improve, and RGIII refuses medical help after eating spoiled guacamole from Subway and dies during the coin flip of their season opener. Their fans start World War III, ending life as we know it.

Can we play a fantasy football version of two lies and a truth?
Sure. One of these points might help you win your fantasy league, two definitely won't.

1. Never take players who have a bye over Halloween weekend like Washington does this year. Between over-partying, candies laced with razor blades, and turned ankles from trick-or-treating, too much can go wrong.

2. RB Alfred Morris' numbers for the last two years haven't been close the great stats he put up as a rookie in 2012. Unless you think things will be different in D.C. this year, I wouldn't draft him with a ten foot pole. (What? Some leagues use poles for drafting.)

3. WR DeSean Jackson wants to be good this season so reach for him in the 3rd round.

Is there anything about this team I don't know that I probably should?
LB Ryan Kerrigan really likes the word 'abrasion.'

Enough nonsense, what's your prediction for this season?
Though probably headed in the right direction, I don't see how this team significantly improves from last year's fiasco. Terrance Knighton bolsters the front of Washington's hybrid 3-4, but the league's worst secondary in 2014 won't be much better. Joe Barry is a slight upgrade at D.C., but only because Jim Haslett was an absolute dumpster fire. The hope of an improved offense, imho, doesn't rest on RGIII, but rather on Bill Callahan's revamped running game. The O-line coach comes over from Dallas, and has brought with him a new blocking scheme that, even if used part-time, could help Alfred Morris (and rookie Matt Jones) excel. I don't know if Jay Gruden will be afforded all the time he needs to turn this around, but I do know it's not happening this year. Oh, and can we change the team name already? How about the Washington Washingtons? Done.

The Pro Football Beast Prediction: **3-13**

Your Genius Prediction: _____

GREEN BAY PACKERS

'14: 12-4 | 1st NFC North | #2 NFC Seed

WK1	@chi	2015 SCHED	
WK 2	SEA	WK 10	DET
WK 3	KC	WK 11	@min
WK 4	@sf	WK 12	CHI
WK 5	STL	WK 13	@det
WK 6	SD	WK 14	DAL
WK 7	BYE	WK 15	@oak
WK 8	@den	WK 16	@ari
WK 9	@car	WK 17	MIN

Claim to Fame: Scored 30.4 PPG, the most in the NFL last year.

Team Anagram to represent last season: Geek Craps Nearby

LOOKING AHEAD TO 2015...

Key Additions: Damarious Randall (draft)... (and re-signing Randall Cobb, Bryan Bulaga, John Kuhn, and B.J. Raji)
Key Subtractions: Tramon Williams (CLE), Dujuan Harris (MIN), AJ Hawk (CIN), Jarrett Boykin (CAR), Davon House (JAX)
Key Multiplication: 8 x 8 = 64
Key Division: 39% of Green Bay's fan base owns a part of the team, 61% own at least three Packers jerseys and a fake-cheese headpiece coated in dandruff.

(HC) Mike McCarthy, 10th yr | **(DC)** Dom Capers, 7th yr | **(OC)** Edgar Bennett, 1st yr
Base Defense: 3-4

EVERYTHING ELSE YOU NEED TO KNOW...

Do they play in London this year?
Nope. Never have, either.

Do they play inside of a candle this year?
Nope. That doesn't make any sense.

How many prime time games are they scheduled for?
Five, including a home game Thanksgiving night against the Bears.

Do you have any other thoughts on their schedule?
Based on last year's records it's the 14th toughest in the league...they have four consecutive division games in 19 days (Weeks 10-14)...four of their first six are at home, so they'll be road warriors down the stretch...in the race for the top seed in the NFC, they get a break in having both Seattle and Dallas come to Lambeau Field...they will be wearing new throwback uniforms for their Week 6 game against the Chargers.

EVERYTHING ELSE YOU NEED TO KNOW (CONT'D)...

What is their best-case and worst-case scenario for the season?
Best case, they go 16-0 and win the Super Bowl. Worst case, global warming escalates so quickly that it is 115 degrees at kickoff of their final game against Minnesota. Delirious from the heat, their fans hallucinate that Aaron Rodgers is wearing Viking purple and riot, starting World War III and ending life as we know it.

Can we play a fantasy football version of two lies and a truth?
Sure. One of these points might help you win your fantasy league, two definitely won't.

1. I plan on walking on for Green Bay's last pre-season game as a wide receiver and making the team. If that happens, draft me as a WR2 in your fantasy league.

2. With some question marks around AP's return and Leveon Bell's 2-game suspension, I'm fine with you taking Eddie Lacy with pick #1. I like him for 1450 yards and 14 TDs.

3. Aaron Rodgers has gone on record as liking over-inflated footballs, but the NFL will be strict about it this year. With regulation balls, I see him throwing for 2 TDs and 149 INTs.

Is there anything about this team I don't know that I probably should?
WR Jordy Nelson has never yawned.

Enough nonsense, what's your prediction for this season?
This team should have been in the Super Bowl last year, so why not bring the whole gang back? New play-caller Tom Clements (promoted from O.C. to Assistant H.C.) has more toys than anyone in the league. If they stay healthy this will be the league's best offense, especially if Davante Adams makes the leap to a stud WR3 behind Nelson/Cobb. The defense hinges on Clay Matthews, who will move between OLB and ILB this year to help bolster the run defense like he did in late 2014. The Pack want to start fast and finish strong, and I think they will, hosting the NFC Championship game in Lambeau.

The Pro Football Beast Prediction: **12-4**

Your Genius Prediction: _____

Predictions from Kickstarter Super Fans...

Michael Wagner | Green Bay, WI - When it's all said and done - Rodgers > Starr > Favre. I play in a Fantasy Football League with "Daddy's Little Princess", a full-grown 6'3" man-child. I'm the Whitney Houston to his Kevin Costner. Hi, Waggy! Go Pack Go! Da Bears Still Suck. PREDICTION: 12-4 and a 5th Lombardi Trophy!

DETROIT LIONS

'14: 11-5 | 2nd NFC North | #6 NFC Seed

WK 1	@sd	2015 SCHED	
WK 2	@min	WK 10	@gb
WK 3	DEN	WK 11	OAK
WK 4	@sea	WK 12	PHL
WK 5	ARI	WK 13	GB
WK 6	CHI	WK 14	@stl
WK 7	MIN	WK 15	@no
WK 8	@kc*	WK 16	SF
WK 9	BYE	WK 17	@chi

Claim to Fame: They had the best rush defense (3.2 yards per attempt) in the league last year.

Team Anagram to represent last season: Driest Lotion

LOOKING AHEAD TO 2015...

Key Additions: Haloti Ngata (BAL), Josh Wilson (ATL), Tyrunn Walker (NO), Laken Tomlinson (draft), Ameer Abdulah (draft)
Key Subtractions: N'Damukung Suh (MIA), Reggie Bush (SF), Nick Fairley (STL), George Johnson (TB), Jed Collins (DAL)
Key Multiplication: 11 x 3 = 33
Key Division: 39% of all Jim Caldwell sideline camera shots show him stone faced, 61% show him rock faced.

(HC) Jim Caldwell, 2nd yr | **(DC)** Teryl Austin, 2nd yr | **(OC)** Joe Lombardi, 2nd yr
Base Defense: 4-3

EVERYTHING ELSE YOU NEED TO KNOW...

Do they play in London this year?
Yes. A Week 8 road game "at Kansas City" at 9:30am ET on Nov. 1st.

Do they play in Vancouver this year?
Nope. The NFL does not play games there, you jackweed.

How many prime time games are they scheduled for?
Four, including back to back vs. Denver and at Seattle in Weeks 3 & 4.

Do you have any other thoughts on their schedule?
Based on last year's records it's the 15th toughest in the league...pretty brutal start with three of the first four on the road...they'll stay warm in December as all their games in that month are indoors...both Packer games happen inside a 19-day window (Weeks 10 & 13) and could determine the eventual division winner.

EVERYTHING ELSE YOU NEED TO KNOW (CONT'D)...

What is their best-case and worst-case scenario for the season?
Best case, they go 16-0 and win the Super Bowl. Worst case, they make the playoffs and face the Cowboys again, only to have a game-winning touchdown taken off the scoreboard when Jerry Jones throws a monogrammed penalty flag onto the field from his luxury box. Incensed, their fans start World War III, ending life as we know it.

Can we play a fantasy football version of two lies and a truth?
Sure. One of these points might help you win your fantasy league, two definitely won't.

1. My sources with the Lions tell me that they have installed anvils in the roof of their dome this year that they will strategically drop onto opposing players at opportune times. Don't start anyone playing on the road in Detroit this year.

2. Golden Tate led all WRs last year with 709 yards after the catch, and I see that number skyrocketing to 7,090 this year because I don't think he will be tackled once in 16 games.

3. Instead of being the first person to draft a defense in the middle rounds, take a flier on an unproven RB like the Lions' Ameer Abdullah. By the time Detroit comes out of their Week 9 bye, he could be the main ball carrier in front of Joique Bell and Theo Riddick.

Is there anything about this team I don't know that I probably should?
Head Coach Jim Caldwell always tries to push out at least one fart during the national anthem, ideally during the phrase, "...bombs bursting in air."

Enough nonsense, what's your prediction for this season?
Of the handful of teams I can't decide which way to go with, Detroit may have the highest ceiling. On the plus side, the coaching staff is solid, the offensive weapons are plentiful, and the defense has a few studs in Haloti Ngata and Ezekiel Ansah. My main issues lie in their QB and their defensive identity. Is Matt Stafford great? His completion percentage on balls thrown at least 15 yards downfield has decreased three seasons in a row, while his interceptions on those passes have risen three straight. That's not good. And how will a defense that was the best against the run last year deal with losing Suh and Fairley? We shall see. On the plus side, watch out for Ameer Abdullah, as he could be a beast. And watch out for a regression from the Lions, especially if they stumble out of the gate and Minnesota lives up to the hype.

The Pro Football Beast Prediction: **9-7**

Your Genius Prediction: _____

MINNESOTA VIKINGS

'14: 7-9 | 3rd NFC North | Missed Playoffs

WK 1	@sf	2015 SCHED	
WK 2	DET	WK 10	@oak
WK 3	SD	WK 11	GB
WK 4	@den	WK 12	@atl
WK 5	BYE	WK 13	SEA
WK 6	KC	WK 14	@ari
WK 7	@det	WK 15	CHI
WK 8	@chi	WK 16	NYG
WK 9	STL	WK 17	@gb

Claim to Fame: No team lost fewer fumbles (only 2!!!) in the NFL last year.

Team Anagram to represent last season: Team Invoking Sins

LOOKING AHEAD TO 2015...

Key Additions: Mike Wallace (MIA), Terence Newman (CIN), Dujuan Harris (GB), Trae Waynes (draft)
Key Subtractions: Greg Jennings (MIA), Matt Cassell (BUF), Jasper Brinkley (DAL)
Key Multiplication: 6 x 8 = 48
Key Division: 39% of the team thought that dress looked blue and black, 61% saw white and gold.

(HC) Mike Zimmer, 2nd yr | **(DC)** George Edwards, 2nd yr | **(OC)** Norv Turner, 2nd yr
Base Defense: 4-3

EVERYTHING ELSE YOU NEED TO KNOW...

Do they play in London this year?
Nope. They beat the Steelers 34-27 in London in 2013.

Do they play in Hong Kong this year?
Nope. The NFL does not play games there, you nincompoop.

How many prime time games are they scheduled for?
Two, including the late Monday Night slot in Week1 at San Francisco.

Do you have any other thoughts on their schedule?
Based on last year's records it's the 12th toughest in the league...they don't play a team that finished last year with a losing record until Week 8 in Chicago... November sets up as their easiest month with games at Chicago, vs. St. Louis, and at Atlanta...barring a playoff run, they'll play their final game at TCF Bank Stadium in Week 16 as they are moving into a brand new stadium next year.

EVERYTHING ELSE YOU NEED TO KNOW (CONT'D)...

What is their best-case and worst-case scenario for the season?
Best case, they go 16-0 and win the Super Bowl. Worst case, their new stadium crumbles to pieces on the day of the ribbon-cutting ceremony and the team announces that they too want to move to Los Angeles. Their fans start World War III, ending life as we know it.

Can we play a fantasy football version of two lies and a truth?
Sure. One of these points might help you win your fantasy league, two definitely won't.

1. Do not draft WR Cris Carter. He retired in 2002.

2. Do not start Teddy Bridgewater in Week 1 at San Francisco. His normal bedtime is 6:15 pm; no way he makes it through a game that doesn't start until 10:30 pm ET.

3. Mike Wallace, perennial downfield threat, played with Ryan Tannehill last year, a QB known for delivering terrible deep balls. Keep an eye on him as a buy-low in your draft.

Is there anything about this team I don't know that I probably should?
Head Coach Mike Zimmer wishes football coaches wore uniforms like baseball managers. For this reason, he rocks a Minnesota Twins uniform under his coaching garb on Sundays.

Enough nonsense, what's your prediction for this season?
Every time Norv Turner tries to sleep, I bet he gets visions of what this offense could be and it makes him giddy. Teddy Bridgewater was a beast last year once given the car keys, leading the NFL in completion percentage on third downs and in the red zone. This year he has an angry Adrian Peterson beside him and another weapon in Mike Wallace. Questions remain in the secondary, but studs like Anthony Barr, Xavier Rhodes, and Harrison Smith have this defense on the rise. It's a tough early schedule, but I think the Vikings make the leap above .500 and live up to the hype.

The Pro Football Beast Prediction: **10-6**

Your Genius Prediction: _____

Predictions from Kickstarter Super Fans...

Ernie Reppe | Eau Claire, WI - I hate that the Vikings have become a trendy sleeper pick. Yes, they have a franchise QB, a hard-nosed coach, and the makings of a top-5 D. And yes, they have AP back with fresh legs. But I still think 2015 will be a developmental year. The biggest question for me is whether or not the Vikes have a go-to WR – a guy Teddy can trust in crunch time. My gut says they don't. PREDICTION: 9-7.

CHICAGO BEARS

'14: 5-11 | 4th NFC North | Missed Playoffs

WK 1	GB	2015 SCHED	
WK 2	ARI	WK 10	@stl
WK 3	@sea	WK 11	DEN
WK 4	OAK	WK 12	@gb
WK 5	@kc	WK 13	SF
WK 6	@det	WK 14	WAS
WK 7	BYE	WK 15	@min
WK 8	MIN	WK 16	@tb
WK 9	@sd	WK 17	DET

Claim to Fame: Gave up 27.6 PPG, the most in the NFC last year.

Team Anagram to represent last season: Grabs a Choice

LOOKING AHEAD TO 2015...

Key Additions: Pernell McPhee (BAL), Mason Foster (TB), Antrel Rolle (NYG), Eddie Royal (SD), Kevin White (draft)
Key Subtractions: Brandon Marshall (NYJ), Stephen Paea (WAS)
Key Multiplication: 4 x 9 = 36
Key Division: 39% of their locker room has wanted to punch Jay Cutler at some point during their career, 61% already have.

(HC) John Fox, 1st yr | **(DC)** Vic Fangio, 1st yr | **(OC)** Adam Gase, 1st yr
Base Defense: 3-4

EVERYTHING ELSE YOU NEED TO KNOW...

Do they play in London this year?
Nope. They beat the Buccaneers in London, 24-18, in 2011.

Do they play in the Sagittarius Dwarf Elliptical Galaxy this year?
Nope. The NFL does not play games there as it is 70,000 light years from the sun.

How many prime time games are they scheduled for?
Two, both of them on the road in the month of November (weeks 9 & 12).

Do you have any other thoughts on their schedule?
Based on last year's records it's the 13th toughest in the league...and it starts with maybe the most difficult three games to open the season of any team this year (vs. GB, vs. ARI, @ SEA)...Week 6 (@DET) and Week 10 (@STL) are their only indoor games...their easiest month of the season looks to be December (weeks 13-16), but by that point will their games even matter? Spoiler alert: they won't...they will wear throwback uniforms for their games in Week 1 and Week 13.

EVERYTHING ELSE YOU NEED TO KNOW (CONT'D)...

What is their best-case and worst-case scenario for the season?
Best case, they go 16-0 and win the Super Bowl. Worst case, Jay Cutler gets benched for throwing seven interceptions in Week 1 and the Bears sign Brett Favre out of retirement. Upon beholding the sight of Favre in a Bears uniform, their fans immediately start World War III, ending life as we know it.

Can we play a fantasy football version of two lies and a truth?
Sure. One of these points might help you win your fantasy league, two definitely won't.

1. Matt Forte doesn't know it yet, but he developed an allergy to pigskin this off-season while working on a hog farm in his hometown of Slidell, LA. Don't draft him.

2. Rookie WR Kevin White has 13-inch fingers on both hands that help him catch everything he can reach. But, before you take him with your first pick, consider that he also has 13-inch arms, so he can't reach anything.

3. Martellus Bennett's 90 receptions led all TEs last year, and this year he's teaming up with new OC Adam Gase, who helped Julius Thomas shine in Denver. If you're not afraid of Jay Cutler (and I don't fault you if you are), Bennett could be a mid-round steal.

Is there anything about this team I don't know that I probably should?
WR Alshon Jeffery had the idea for Clash of Clans in 2010. His game was called Tussle of Tribes and it would have made him billions. He cries himself to sleep every night.

Enough nonsense, what's your prediction for this season?
Can new Offensive Coordinator Adam Gase revive Cutler's career? Maybe, but it's going to take more than year to do it. I think Kevin White will live up to the hype, but the problem for Jay Cutler has never been a lack of weapons, has it? (If Gase does make it happen off the bat, he may get the head coaching gig some say he already deserves.) Over on defense, Vic Fangio is the right man for the job, but he'll need some time to get the right players in house for his 3-4 defense. There will be a learning curve, and Chicago will pay in the form of losses, early and often. If I'm a Bears fan, I'm not too happy about the John Fox hire, but I've never been a fan of his. I'd also be circling December on my calendar and praying for a 3-1 finish to give us momentum going into next year. It's one step back in 2015, and maybe, in 2016, two steps forward.

The Pro Football Beast Prediction: **4-12**

Your Genius Prediction: _____

CAROLINA PANTHERS

'14: 7-8-1 | 1st NFC South | #4 NFC Seed

WK 1	@jax	2015 SCHED	
WK 2	HOU	WK 10	@ten
WK 3	NO	WK 11	WAS
WK 4	@tb	WK 12	@dal
WK 5	BYE	WK 13	@no
WK 6	@sea	WK 14	ATL
WK 7	PHL	WK 15	@nyg
WK 8	IND	WK 16	@atl
WK 9	GB	WK 17	TB

Claim to Fame: They made the playoffs with a losing record. #shameful

Team Anagram to represent last season:
No Ripe Charlatans

LOOKING AHEAD TO 2015...

Key Additions: Charles Tillman (CHI), Jordan Todman (JAX), Jarrett Boykin (GB), Michael Oher (TEN), Shaq Thompson (draft)
Key Subtractions: DeAngelo Williams (PIT), Greg Hardy (DAL)
Key Multiplication: 4 x 0 = 0
Key Division: 39% of the team likes black licorice, the other 61% doesn't understand why a word pronounced "lickerish" is spelled "licorice."

(HC) Ron Rivera, 5th yr | **(DC)** Sean McDermott, 5th yr | **(OC)** Mike Shula, 3rd yr
Base Defense: 4-3

EVERYTHING ELSE YOU NEED TO KNOW...

Do they play in London this year?
Nope. Never have, either.

Do they play in West Carolina this year?
Nope. That is not a state, Einstein.

How many prime time games are they scheduled for?
Two, back to back in Weeks 7 and 8. They lost back to back prime time games last year.

Do you have any other thoughts on their schedule?
Based on last year's records it's the 6th easiest in the league...no team might have a better shot of starting the season 4-0 with games at JAX, vs. HOU, vs. NO, and at TB...the back end of their schedule isn't much tougher, with their final five games coming against teams that finished 8-8 or worse last year...they'll be looking to avenge a prime time loss to Philly last year when they meet in Week 7 on Sunday night.

EVERYTHING ELSE YOU NEED TO KNOW (CONT'D)...

What is their best-case and worst-case scenario for the season?
Best case, they go 16-0 and win the Super Bowl. Worst case, all of their games end in a tie and they finish 0-0-16. Frustrated by the lack of winning or losing, and even more so by the constant use of the phrase, "it's like kissing your sister," their fans start World War III, ending life as we know it.

Can we play a fantasy football version of two lies and a truth?
Sure. One of these points might help you win your fantasy league, two definitely won't.

1. Tired of drafting DeAngelo Williams only to watch his production be stymied by injuries and Jonathan Stewart? He's coming off a broken hand and he's not even on this team anymore so why are we even talking about him? Let's move on.

2. Tired of drafting Jonathan Stewart only to watch his production be stymied by injuries and DeAngelo Williams? While I can't guarantee his health, he's no longer sharing the backfield with Williams. I think this is the year he lives up to the hype as a solid RB2.

3. Tired of drafting Luke Kuechly as your quarterback? You should be. He's a linebacker.

Is there anything about this team I don't know that I probably should?
Cam Newton's new $103MM contract includes a $10K bonus each game for appearing on camera on the sidelines doing that ridiculous thing where he drapes a towel over his head and tucks it into his shoulder pads. At least now we know why he does it.

Enough nonsense, what's your prediction for this season?
There's usually nothing wrong with bringing back a team that's won its division two years in a row, but I'm not buying it with these Panthers. There's a lack of depth across this roster that could spell trouble if any of their big names lose time to injury. Kuechly is the class of the league at LB, and I expect good things from Jonathan Stewart until he gets injured, but let's not forget how 2014 played out. This team won a total of one game in October AND November last year before beating four under-.500 teams to barely make the playoffs. I think the rest of the South will be better across the board, so even if the Panthers make it to .500, it's not getting them into the playoffs. I know I'm in the minority by predicting them to miss the post-season, but just like Uncle Jesse in that episode of *Full House* where he rides his motorcycle on the roof of a building to prove he can still live up to his nickname of Dr. Dare, I live on the edge.

The Pro Football Beast Prediction: **8-8**

Your Genius Prediction: _____

NEW ORLEANS SAINTS

'14: 7-9 | 2nd NFC South | Missed Playoffs

WK 1	@ari	2015 SCHED	
WK 2	TB	WK 10	@was
WK 3	@car	WK 11	BYE
WK 4	DAL	WK 12	@hou
WK 5	@phl	WK 13	CAR
WK 6	ATL	WK 14	@tb
WK 7	@ind	WK 15	DET
WK 8	NYG	WK 16	JAX
WK 9	TEN	WK 17	@atl

Claim to Fame: Their offense led the league in yards per game (411.4) last year.

Team Anagram to represent last season:
Serial Wantonness

LOOKING AHEAD TO 2015...

Key Additions: Brandon Browner (NE), C.J. Spiller (BUF), Kyle Wilson (NYJ), Kevin Williams (SEA), Andrus Peat (draft)
Key Subtractions: Jimmy Graham (SEA), Kenny Stills (MIA), Patrick Robinson (SD), Junior Gallette (FA), Pierre Thomas (FA)
Key Multiplication: 13 x 3 = 39
Key Division: 39% of their fan base has no idea what a 'fleur-de-lis' is, the other 61% pense que vous êtes un idiot laid.

(HC) Sean Payton, 10th yr | **(DC)** Rob Ryan, 3rd yr | **(OC)** Pete Carmichael Jr., 7th yr
Base Defense: 3-4

EVERYTHING ELSE YOU NEED TO KNOW...

Do they play in London this year?
Nope. They beat the Chargers, 37-32, in London in 2008.

Do they play in Moscow this year?
Nope. The NFL does not play games there, comrade.

How many prime time games are they scheduled for?
Three, and they are all at home.

Do you have any other thoughts on their schedule?
Based on last year's records it's the 5th easiest in the league...they never have to play road games on back to back weeks...they get a late bye week this year (Week 11)...their last "cold outdoors" game of the regular season is on November 15th at Washington...makes you wonder if the NFL is paying reparations to the Saints for Sean Payton's suspension with a cake schedule this year?

EVERYTHING ELSE YOU NEED TO KNOW (CONT'D)...

What is their best-case and worst-case scenario for the season?
Best case, they go 16-0 and win the Super Bowl. Worst case, Roger Goodell suspends Sean Payton for the 2011 BountyGate incident again because "it just feels right in my artificial heart that is made of carbon, graphene, and unicorn sinew." Unamused with the commish, their fans start World War III, ending life as we know it.

Can we play a fantasy football version of two lies and a truth?
Sure. One of these points might help you win your fantasy league, two definitely won't.

1. Rumor has it that CJ Spiller's birth certificate is a fake and his actual date of birth is 1947, not 1987. Do not draft this 68-year old relic of an athlete.

2. Brandin Cooks is being drafted early in the fifth round of fantasy mocks this year, and with good reason. With Graham and Stills out of N.O., he should see a ton of targets this season. Don't reach for him in the fourth, but if he's there with your fifth pick, take him.

3. The Saints Defense will pick off every Hail Mary attempt this year and return them all for touchdowns. Selecting them in the second round is a no-brainer.

Is there anything about this team I don't know that I probably should?
To stay loose before games the team plays Duck-Duck-Goose in their locker room.

Enough nonsense, what's your prediction for this season?
I love that they overhauled their offense. Gone are the four players who caught 51% of all Drew Brees' passes last year (Graham, Stills, Thomas, and Cadet), and while they'll miss Graham in the red zone, it sounds like he was a locker room issue, so...good riddance. I like Spiller to have a monster year, and ditto for Brandin Cooks, who shined in 10 games last year before an injury. Brandon Browner, Anthony Spencer, and Kyle Wilson aren't enough to makeover the Saints' 31st-ranked defense, but coupling their additions with the new, simpler scheme the Saints are installing this year will help New Orleans improve on their bottom-10 finishes in sacks, interceptions, and forced fumbles. On the flip side, they let Junior Gallette go for off-field reasons this summer, a move that not only hurt their defense, but also means that almost 20% of their cap space is being paid to guys not on the roster. I'm not sure you can overcome that in this league, so while I think the Saints get back to .500 or better on sheer talent and an easy schedule, I think they just miss out on the post-season.

The Pro Football Beast Prediction: **9-7**

Your Genius Prediction: _____

ATLANTA FALCONS

'14: 6-10 | 3rd NFC South | Missed Playoffs

WK1	PHL	2015 SCHED	
WK 2	@nyg	WK 10	BYE
WK 3	@dal	WK 11	IND
WK 4	HOU	WK 12	MIN
WK 5	WAS	WK 13	@tb
WK 6	@no	WK 14	@car
WK 7	@ten	WK 15	@jax
WK 8	TB	WK 16	CAR
WK 9	@sf	WK 17	NO

Claim to Fame: Finished last in 2014 in yards allowed and third-down defense.

Team Anagram to represent last season: Fatal Snot Canal

LOOKING AHEAD TO 2015...

Key Additions: Brooks Reed (HOU), Justin Durant (DAL), Adrian Clayborn (TB), Chris Chester (WAS), Jacob Tamme (DEN), Vic Beasley (draft)
Key Subtractions: Corey Peters (ARI), Sean Weatherspoon (ARI), Josh Wilson (DET)
Key Multiplication: 12 x 1 = 12
Key Division: 39% of their team loved being on HBO's Hard Knocks last year, the other 61% thought they were on documentary called, "Let's Get Mike Smith Fired."

(HC) Dan Quinn, 1st yr | **(DC)** Richard Smith, 1st yr | **(OC)** Kyle Shanahan, 1st yr
Base Defense: 4-3

EVERYTHING ELSE YOU NEED TO KNOW...

Do they play in London this year?
Nope. They lost in heartbreaking fashion to the Lions in London last year, 22-21.

Do they play in Paris this year?
Nope. The NFL does not play games there, you chain-smoking, baguette-eating jerk.

How many prime time games are they scheduled for?
Two, including the early Monday Night game in Week 1.

Do you have any other thoughts on their schedule?
Based on last year's records it's the #1 easiest schedule in the league...three straight games against the NFC East to open the season is an interesting twist...if new HC Dan Quinn plays his former team (Seattle) this year, it will have to be in a playoff matchup... four of their last five are against division opponents (including playing the Panthers twice in December), setting up what could be a great playoff race in the NFC South.

EVERYTHING ELSE YOU NEED TO KNOW (CONT'D)...

What is their best-case and worst-case scenario for the season?
Best case, they go 16-0 and win the Super Bowl. Worst case, in lieu of pumping in fake crowd noise (like they have the past two seasons) they pump in a flock of rabid peregrine falcons who escape the stadium, breed with robots, create a master race of rabid falconbots that attack humans and start World War III, ending life as we know it.

Can we play a fantasy football version of two lies and a truth?
Sure. One of these points might help you win your fantasy league, two definitely won't.

1. Want to make this the most memorable fantasy draft EVER? Take the Falcons Defense with your first pick and announce, "You peons will never forget the year I took the Falcons Defense with my first pick and still won the league!" If you go on to win the league, you will live on in infamy. If you don't, at least everyone has a great story.

2. New O.C. Kyle Shanahan thought Julio Jones gave him a dirty look when the two met at OTAs this summer. Expect Shanahan to call zero plays for Julio until they confront the issue in a peer mediation session in early October. Do not draft.

3. Rookie RB Tevin Coleman is currently being drafted five rounds ahead of Devonta Freeman, who is going early in the 12th round. Coleman has more upside, but don't sleep on Freeman, who could be a late-draft steal.

Is there anything about this team I don't know that I probably should?
They call him "Matty Ice" because of a rare small intestine issue he's had since birth that causes his feces to come out frozen.

Enough nonsense, what's your prediction for this season?
Over the last two years this team was 5-11 in close games, including disasters like their Week 8 loss to the Lions at Wembley Stadium last year. It was time for a change, and change has come. This defense, the worst in the league in 2014, gets bolstered by a new coordinator, a new head coach who used to run Seattle's defense, and a solid draft class. Despite persistent O-line issues, Kyle Shanahan will make this offense better, especially in the run game where the Falcons were among the league's worst last year. Look for rookie Tevin Coleman to break out and Matt Ryan to put up career numbers. Every year we get surprised by an over-achiever that makes the playoffs, and thanks to a coaching upgrade and a cream-puff schedule, I'm taking the dirty birds to rise up and do just that.

The Pro Football Beast Prediction: **9-7**

Your Genius Prediction: _____

TAMPA BAY BUCCANEERS

'14: 2-14 | 4th in NFC South | Missed Playoffs

WK1	TEN	2015 SCHED	
WK 2	@no	WK 10	DAL
WK 3	@hou	WK 11	@phl
WK 4	CAR	WK 12	@ind
WK 5	JAX	WK 13	ATL
WK 6	BYE	WK 14	NO
WK 7	@was	WK 15	@stl
WK 8	@atl	WK 16	CHI
WK 9	NYG	WK 17	@car

Claim to Fame: Scored 17.3 PPG, the fewest in the NFC last year.

Team Anagram to represent last season:
Scam Crap Beauty Bean

LOOKING AHEAD TO 2015...

Key Additions: Bruce Carter (DAL), George Johnson (DET), Henry Melton (DAL), Chris Conte (CHI), Jamies Winston (draft)
Key Subtractions: Mason Foster (CHI), Dashon Goldson (WAS), Adrian Clayborn (ATL)
Key Multiplication: 7 x 6 = 42
Key Division: 39% of their fans can't spell the word 'Buccaneers', the other 61% can't spell 'Tampa Bay'.

(HC) Lovie Smith, 2nd yr | **(DC)** Leslie Frazier, 2nd yr | **(OC)** Dirk Koetter, 1st yr
Base Defense: 4-3

EVERYTHING ELSE YOU NEED TO KNOW...

Do they play in London this year?
Nope. They are 0-2 in London, losing to the Patriots in 2009 and the Bears in 2011.

Do they play at the North Pole this year?
Nope. The NFL does not play games there, you cotton-headed ninny muggins.

How many prime time games are they scheduled for?
One, at St. Louis on a Thursday night in Week 15.

Do you have any other thoughts on their schedule?
Based on last year's records it's the 4th easiest in the league...they have 13 of their 16 games in the early afternoon Sunday slot...Week 1 features a fun matchup vs. Mariota should they both start...after Week 1, the Bucs have a rare pattern of two road games followed by two home games that repeats three times in a row up through Week 14...four of their first five games after their Week 6 bye are against the NFC East.

EVERYTHING ELSE YOU NEED TO KNOW (CONT'D)...

What is their best-case and worst-case scenario for the season?
Best case, they go 16-0 and win the Super Bowl. Worst case, Jamies Winston quits on Labor Day to take a lucrative offer from Red Lobster to start his own franchise of Famous Jamies' Crab Shacks. He also hires away backup QB Mike Glennon as his shift manager. Forced to watch second-year QB Seth Lobato run the offense, their fans revolt and start World War III, ending life as we know it.

Can we play a fantasy football version of two lies and a truth?
Sure. One of these points might help you win your fantasy league, two definitely won't.

1. Doug Martin finally went through puberty this off-season and should put up great numbers as a result.

2. Don't be afraid to grab WR Mike Evans with your third round pick this year. He has the size and talent to improve on his 12-TD rookie campaign, he will be used for more deep routes this year, and the Bucs will be behind in plenty of games and looking to throw.

3. Not a single winning fantasy team in all of the U.S. last year had a Bucs player on it.

Is there anything about this team I don't know that I probably should?
LB Lavonte David has never died.

Enough nonsense, what's your prediction for this season?
They've been a sneaky sleeper pick each of the last two years, only to combine for a 6-26 record. Ouch. Though they've added Jameis Winston this year, the buzz seems to be quieter, and with good reason: there are major issues on both sides of the ball. Jameis will improve their passing game, but don't expect much from the run game. Dirk Koetter's ground game was impotent in Atlanta, and here in Florida he has subpar backs and the league's worst offensive line. Leaders abound on defense, and having a year of Lovie Smith's system under their belt should lead to better results. No team was worse in close games in 2014 (1-8), so there's nowhere to go but up. Unfortunately for Tampa Bay fans, it's not much more than a baby step.

The Pro Football Beast Prediction: **5-11**

Your Genius Prediction: _____

Predictions from Kickstarter Super Fans...

Michael Stoltzfus | Lancaster, PA - PREDICTION: 5-11

SEATTLE SEAHAWKS

'14: 12-4 | 1st NFC West | #1 NFC Seed

WK1	@stl	2015 SCHED	
WK 2	@gb	WK 10	ARI
WK 3	CHI	WK 11	SF
WK 4	DET	WK 12	PIT
WK 5	@cin	WK 13	@min
WK 6	CAR	WK 14	@bal
WK 7	@sf	WK 15	CLE
WK 8	@dal	WK 16	STL
WK 9	BYE	WK 17	@ari

Claim to Fame: Gave up 15.9 PPG, fewest in the NFL in 2014. Oh, and that play call.

Team Anagram to represent last season:
Awake. Lash Testes.

LOOKING AHEAD TO 2015...

Key Additions: Jimmy Graham (NO), Cary Williams (PHL), Will Blackmon (JAX), Tyler Lockett (draft)
Key Subtractions: Byron Maxwell (PHL), Malcolm Smith (OAK), James Carpenter (NYJ), Max Unger (NO), Jeron Johnson (WAS), Kevin Williams (NO)
Key Multiplication: 9 x 9 = 81
Key Division: 39% of their locker room thinks they probably should have handed off to Marshawn, the other 61% knows they should have handed off to Marshawn.

(HC) Pete Carroll, 6th yr | **(DC)** Kris Richard, 1st yr | **(OC)** Darrell Bevell, 5th yr
Base Defense: 4-3

EVERYTHING ELSE YOU NEED TO KNOW...

Do they play in London this year?
Nope. Never have, either.

Do they play in Venice this year?
Nope. The NFL does not play games there, you bridge troll.

How many prime time games are they scheduled for?
Five, including three Sunday nights, one Monday night, and one Thursday night.

Do you have any other thoughts on their schedule?
Based on last year's records it's the 4th toughest in the league...they have nine games against playoff teams from last year...five of their eight road games are against teams who finished with double digit wins last year...three straight home games after the bye should set them up for another playoff run down the stretch.

EVERYTHING ELSE YOU NEED TO KNOW (CONT'D)...

What is their best-case and worst-case scenario for the season?
Best case, they go 16-0 and win the Super Bowl. Worst case, they go 16-0, make the Super Bowl, and have the ball down by four with 3 seconds left on the 1-yard line and hand the ball to Marshawn Lynch and he takes a knee and says, "NOW you give it to me," and they lose. Their fans start World War III, ending life as we know it.

Can we play a fantasy football version of two lies and a truth?
Sure. One of these points might help you win your fantasy league, two definitely won't.

1. Do not draft Jimmy Graham. It's well documented that he is afraid of loud noises, and it's going to lead to him averaging 1.1 catches for 4.2 yards in all of his home games this year because of that raucous Seattle crowd. Terrible move by the Seattle brass.

2. Everybody's had Marshawn Lynch on their team before, so he's not going in the Top 5 in most leagues. If you're picking in that 5-7 range in the first round, draft him and feel great about it, knowing he could finish the year as the league's best back.

3. With your last pick in the draft, take "Seattle's 12th man." Some idiot will tell you, "Dude, the Seahawks D was taken an hour ago," at which point you can say, "I'm drafting their fans, not their defense, moron. Work on your listening skills." After a few seconds of blank stares and awkward silence say, "Fine, just give me the Browns' Defense."

Is there anything about this team I don't know that I probably should?
Pete Carroll is such a prolific gum chewer, he is on his seventh jaw.

Enough nonsense, what's your prediction for this season?
Oh what a difference a play call makes. We could be talking about what it will take for this team to be the first ever to win three in a row, instead we're wondering if that last-second gaffe will have lingering effects on the 2015 season. Make no mistake, this team is still great. Many feel it's the most well run organization in the league from top to bottom. The roster is deep, and the leadership of Pete Carroll and Wilson remains strong. Jimmy Graham adds a new element to their offense, which will continue to be good enough. Replacing Byron Maxwell with Cary Williams is a downgrade, but the front seven remains mostly in tact and Richard Sherman and Earl Thomas will keep the secondary elite if they can shake early health concerns. It's boring to predict it, but I see another NFC West crown and a very deep playoff run for Russell and company.

The Pro Football Beast Prediction: **11-5**

Your Genius Prediction: _____

ARIZONA CARDINALS

'14: 11-5 | 2nd NFC West | #5 NFC Seed

		2015 SCHED	
WK 1	NO		
WK 2	@chi	WK 10	@sea
WK 3	SF	WK 11	CIN
WK 4	STL	WK 12	@sf
WK 5	@det	WK 13	@stl
WK 6	@pit	WK 14	MIN
WK 7	BAL	WK 15	@phi
WK 8	@cle	WK 16	GB
WK 9	BYE	WK 17	SEA

Claim to Fame: Their defense racked up 1,192 penalty yards in 2014, most in the NFL.

Team Anagram to represent last season:
Czar Ordains a Nail

LOOKING AHEAD TO 2015...

Key Additions: Mike Iupati (SF), Sean Weatherspoon (ATL), Corey Peters (ATL), Jermaine Gresham (CIN), D.J. Humphries (draft)
Key Subtractions: Darnell Dockett (SF), Antonio Cromartie (NYJ), Dan Williams (OAK), Lyle Sendlein (FA), Larry Foote (retired)
Key Multiplication: 11 x 1 = 11
Key Division: 39% of their fan base thinks they can win it all with Carson Palmer at QB, the other 61% thinks they can win it all with Carson Daly at QB.

(HC) Bruce Arians, 3rd yr | **(DC)** James Bettcher, 1st yr | **(OC)** Harold Goodwin, 3rd yr
Base Defense: 3-4

EVERYTHING ELSE YOU NEED TO KNOW...

Do they play in London this year?
Nope. Never have, either.

Do they play on a floating barge in the Atlantic Ocean this year?
Nope, but that's not a bad idea. (It's a terrible idea.)

How many prime time games are they scheduled for?
Three, including a big one at Seattle after their bye week.

Do you have any other thoughts on their schedule?
Based on last year's records it's the 5th toughest in the league...they will be road warriors in the middle of the season, with only two home games from Week 5 through Week 13...five of their last seven games are indoors...despite being home, finishing with Green Bay and Seattle is a tough way to close the season if you're fighting for a playoff berth.

EVERYTHING ELSE YOU NEED TO KNOW (CONT'D)...

What is their best-case and worst-case scenario for the season?
Best case, they go 16-0 and win the Super Bowl. Worst case, they suffer twice as many QB injuries as last year, Kurt Warner un-retires, and gets hit on his first drop back and crumbles to death. Despondent, their fans start World War III, ending life as we know it.

Can we play a fantasy football version of two lies and a truth?
How about I just give you one truth?

1. As of this writing Michael Floyd is being drafted, on average, slightly ahead of Larry FItzgerald in the 11th round. I might be crazy, but I disagree. If you're choosing between these two, take the 32-year old who's out to prove he deserved his new 2-year contract.

Is there anything about this team I don't know that I probably should?
CB Patrick Patterson stays sharp in the offseason by catching small woodland creatures with his bare hands while wearing roller skates and a cloth blindfold soaked in acid.

Enough nonsense, what's your prediction for this season?
It's hard to argue with the job Bruce Arians has done. His 21-11 record is impressive, but even more so is the 16-6 mark he's had when Carson Palmer is his leading passer. QB injuries derailed them in 2014, but Palmer is back with an improved offensive line ready for Week 1. The running game remains the question; only the Raiders were worse on the ground in 2014. James Bettcher replaces Todd Bowles as the D.C., but not much will change with their 3-4 scheme. Sean Witherspoon will shine on defense, and Arians will once again have this team believing and winning well into December. Their tough schedule might keep them from double digit wins, but I think they sneak back into the playoffs with a decent chance to win on the road in round one.

The Pro Football Beast Prediction: **10-6**

Your Genius Prediction: _____

Prediction from Scott Allen (on Twitter at @azsportsguy & @raisingzona)...

Scott Allen | Phoenix, AZ - Following their best season since moving to the desert in 1988, I expect the Cardinals to be even better in 2015 as long as they stay healthy. Carson Palmer returns with his same weapons, plus rookie RB David Johnson and TE Jermaine Gresham. The defense changed coordinators but kept the new hire in-house and they should be stronger as well. The biggest upgrade is on the offensive line with the additions of guard Mike Iupati and rookie tackle D.J. Humphries. PREDICTION: 11-5 and a playoff berth in the always-tough NFC West.

SAN FRANCISCO 49ERS

'14: 8-8 | 3rd NFC West | Missed Playoffs

WK 1	MIN	2015 SCHED	
WK 2	@pit	WK 10	BYE
WK 3	@ari	WK 11	@sea
WK 4	GB	WK 12	ARI
WK 5	@nyg	WK 13	@chi
WK 6	BAL	WK 14	@cle
WK 7	SEA	WK 15	CIN
WK 8	@stl	WK 16	@det
WK 9	ATL	WK 17	STL

Claim to Fame: They tallied 191.4 passing yards/game last year, fewest in the NFC.

Team Anagram to represent last season: 49 Fancier Son Scars

LOOKING AHEAD TO 2015...

Key Additions: Reggie Bush (SF), Torrey Smith (BAL), Darnell Dockett (ARI), Phillip Wheeler (MIA), Arik Armstead (draft)
Key Subtractions: Frank Gore (IND), Mike Iupati (ARI), Chris Culliver (WAS), Michael Crabtree (OAK), Dan Skuta (JAX), Chris Borland (retired), Anthony Davis (retired), Justin Smith (retired), Patrick Willis (retired), Jim Harbaugh's Khakis (UM)
Key Multiplication: 8 x 5 = 40
Key Division: 39% of their locker room hated Jim Harbaugh, the other 61% progressed three stages beyond hate into an emotion that there is no word for yet.

(HC) Jim Tomsula, 1st yr | **(DC)** Eric Mangini, 1st yr | **(OC)** Geep Chryst, 1st yr
Base Defense: 3-4

EVERYTHING ELSE YOU NEED TO KNOW...

Do they play in London this year?
Nope. They are 2-0 in London, beating the Broncos in 2010 and the Jaguars in 2013

Do they play in Santa Clara this year?
Yes. They play eight games there because that's where their stadium is.

How many prime time games are they scheduled for?
Four, including hosting the Vikings in the late Monday Night opener in Week 1.

Do you have any other thoughts on their schedule?
Based on last year's records it's the 3rd toughest in the league...three of their four road games after the Week 10 bye could feature cold weather (Seattle, Cleveland, and Chicago)...they have only one division game in their first six weeks and only one in their final five weeks...they face their former D.C., Vic Fangio, in Chicago in Week 13.

EVERYTHING ELSE YOU NEED TO KNOW (CONT'D)...

What is their best-case and worst-case scenario for the season?
Best case, they go 16-0 and win the Super Bowl. Worst case, they go 0-16, the rest of their defense retires, Colin Kaepernick quits to play baseball, and Jim Harbaugh goes undefeated at Michigan and wins the National Title, causing their fans start World War III, ending life as we know it.

Can we play a fantasy football version of two lies and a truth?
Sure. One of these points might help you win your fantasy league, two definitely won't.

1. New fantasy draft rule: if you can't spell a player's name, you can't draft him. Wait until Kaepernick or Roethlisberger get drafted to announce this rule, force the issue with the other owners, and prepare to be assaulted within inches of your life.

2. Looking for a deep sleeper with your last pick? How about Godfrey Jefferson, a player who doesn't even exist.

3. Someone in your league is going to take Carlos Hyde as their RB2. Go ahead and let them. The Niners O-line is in flux and they could be behind in a lot of games. I'd prefer Jonathan Stewart or Melvin Gordon, who are being drafted in the same area.

Is there anything about this team I don't know that I probably should?
In his first move as head coach, Jim Tomsula grilled and ate an entire pair of khakis to signify the team moving on from the Jim Harbaugh era. He has yet to pass them.

Enough nonsense, what's your prediction for this season?
No team has more storylines going into 2015 than the Niners. Harbaugh is gone, the new coach might be crazy, everyone is retiring, and Colin Kaepernick changed his delivery. (Oh, and as this book went to press Aldon Smith got into legal trouble again!) I'm not convinced Tomsula will work, especially with the personnel changes on defense, but the Kaepernick thing could be interesting. Does a new motion from a wider base really change things, or will his numbers continue to decline? He's got new coaches and new weapons, but I see more of the same. I'm also not a fan of their schedule as seven of their first eleven games are tough (SEA twice, ARI twice, GB, BAL, and PIT). They feel like the mirror image of the Vikings - two teams headed in opposite directions - which makes their Week 1 matchup on MNF so intriguing. Super Bowl 50 is in Santa Clara on February 7th, but unless they've got a ticket, the Niners' players certainly won't be.

The Pro Football Beast Prediction: **5-11**

Your Prediction: _____

ST. LOUIS RAMS

'14: 6-10 | 4th NFC West | Missed Playoffs

WK1	SEA	**2015 SCHED**	
WK 2	@was	**WK 10**	CHI
WK 3	PIT	**WK 11**	@bal
WK 4	@ari	**WK 12**	@cin
WK 5	@gb	**WK 13**	ARI
WK 6	BYE	**WK 14**	DET
WK 7	CLE	**WK 15**	TB
WK 8	SF	**WK 16**	@SEA
WK 9	@min	**WK 17**	@SF

Claim to Fame: Their offense racked up 1,139 penalty yards in 2014, most in the NFL.

Team Anagram to represent last season: Turmoil Sass

LOOKING AHEAD TO 2015...

Key Additions: Nick Fairley (DET), Nick Foles (PHL), Akeem Ayers (NE), Todd Gurley (draft)
Key Subtractions: Sam Bradford (PHL), Zac Stacy (NYJ)
Key Multiplication: 21 x 1 = 21
Key Division: 39% of Jeff Fisher's mustache is real, the other 61% comes from a push broom he stole from the Tennessee Titans in 2001.

(HC) Jeff Fisher, 4th yr | **(DC)** Gregg Williams, 2nd yr | **(OC)** Frank Cignetti Jr., 1st yr
Base Defense: 4-3

EVERYTHING ELSE YOU NEED TO KNOW...

Do they play in London this year?
Nope. They lost to the Patriots in London, 45-7, back in 2012

Do they play in Stockholm this year?
Nope. The NFL does not play games there, you cretin.

How many prime time games are they scheduled for?
One, hosting Tampa Bay on a Thursday night in Week 15.

Do you have any other thoughts on their schedule?
Based on last year's records it's the 6th toughest in the league...they open the season hosting Seattle, whom they've beaten at home two of the last three years...thanks to the reduction in his suspension, they won't miss Le'Veon Bell, who will return to action for their matchup in Week 3...they get a rare trifecta of consecutive home games to start December...they'll be home for a month straight thanks to having two home games after their Week 6 bye.

EVERYTHING ELSE YOU NEED TO KNOW (CONT'D)...

What is their best-case and worst-case scenario for the season?
Best case, they go 16-0 and win the Super Bowl. Worst case, they move the team to Los Angeles and THEN they go 16-0, causing their fans to tear down the arch, carry it to California, and use it to start World War III, ending life as we know it.

Can we play a fantasy football version of two lies and a truth?
Sure. One of these points might help you win your fantasy league, two definitely won't.

1. If you won a keeper league last year, when the time comes to announce your keeper for 2015, state that instead of keeping a player you are keeping the championship. By law the league must honor it, and everyone just goes home angry and waits for 2016.

2. Unless you're in a dynasty league, this is not the year to draft Todd Gurley. You're going to have to spend a 6th round (or better) pick on him, and he's running behind a bad offensive line on a recovering knee. He could be great, but wait for next year.

3. If you draft WR Brian Quick this year, send him a handwritten letter letting him know that he's on your team. He saves every letter he gets from fantasy owners in a box under his bed labeled 'Letters from my mom and fantasy owners."

Is there anything about this team I don't know that I probably should?
Kicker Greg Zuerlein hasn't driven a car in over eight years as he believes using the gas and brake pedals, "steal trace amounts of kicking power from my moneymaker." He has a full-time driver and no friends.

Enough nonsense, what's your prediction for this season?
How about this defensive front? Five first-round draft picks with the addition of Nick Fairley this off-season has made the league's best line even better. Though there's room for improvement against the run, their dominating front seven gives them a chance to win every game. The question this year, like last year, is will the offense step up? Answering that question now is Frank Cignetti Jr., who takes over at O.C. for the underwhelming Brian Schottenheimer. He'll start the year with Foles at QB, and he'll end the year with Gurley at RB, but his biggest challenge may be getting more out of Tavon Austin, their undersized burner who hasn't produced in two seasons. In a QB-led league I need to see more from Foles before I pencil them in for the playoffs, but they just might surprise me.

The Pro Football Beast Prediction: **7-9**

Your Genius Prediction: _____

NEW ENGLAND PATRIOTS

'14: 12-4 | 1st AFC East | #1 AFC Seed

Claim to Fame: Won the stinking Super Bowl

Team Anagram to represent last season:
Landowners Get Paint

WK 1	PIT	2015 SCHED	
WK 2	@buf	WK 10	@nyg
WK 3	JAX	WK 11	BUF
WK 4	BYE	WK 12	@den
WK 5	@dal	WK 13	PHL
WK 6	@ind	WK 14	@hou
WK 7	NYJ	WK 15	TEN
WK 8	MIA	WK 16	@nyj
WK 9	WAS	WK 17	@mia

LOOKING AHEAD TO 2015...

Key Additions: Jabaal Sheard (CLE), Bradley Fletcher (PHL), Fred Davis (WAS), Travaris Cadet (NO), Malcom Brown (draft)
Key Subtractions: Vince Wilfork (HOU), Darrelle Revis (NYJ), Brandon Browner (NO), Shane Vereen (NYG), Akeem Ayers (STL), Stevan Ridley (NYJ)
Key Multiplication: $0 \times 0 = 0$
Key Division: 39% of their balls may have been slightly under-inflated last year, the other 61% were filled with Argon gas. I feel like we don't talk enough about Argon these days.

(HC) Bill Belicheck, 16th yr | **(DC)** Matt Patricia, 4th yr | **(OC)** Josh McDaniels, 4th yr
Base Defense: 3-4

EVERYTHING ELSE YOU NEED TO KNOW...

Do they play in London this year?
Nope. They are 2-0 in London, beating Tampa Bay in 2009 and St. Louis in 2012.

Do they play as inmates in a maximum security prison this year?
Nope, though Roger Goodell did try to make that happen.

How many prime time games are they scheduled for?
Five, including the opening Thursday night of the season hosting Pittsburgh.

Do you have any other thoughts on their schedule?
Based on last year's records it's the 11th easiest in the league....their most difficult travel stretch will be heading to Dallas and Indianapolis in back to back weeks...on the flip side, between October 19th and Thanksgiving the only trip they have to make is down the road to the Meadowlands...their traditionally tough game at Miami comes in Week 17.

EVERYTHING ELSE YOU NEED TO KNOW (CONT'D)...

What is their best-case and worst-case scenario for the season?
Best case, they go 16-0 and win the Super Bowl. Worst case, Tom Brady takes the field in Uggs, which causes Twitter to literally blow up the world, ending life as we know it.

Can we play a fantasy football version of two lies and a truth?
Sure. One of these points might help you win your fantasy league, two definitely won't.

1. Whether Jimmy Garoppolo starts 1 or 11 games for the Patriots this year, you want him on your team as your QB1 if your league counts handsomeness as a statistical category.

2. Avoid K Stephen Gostkowski this year as could be abducted by aliens.

3. Bill Belicheck loves nothing more than to screw over your fantasy team. Never, under any circumstances, find yourself with one of his running backs on your roster. NEVER!

Is there anything about this team I don't know that I probably should?
When Bill Belicheck gets tickled his natural reaction is dry heaves and cold sweats.

Enough nonsense Bryan, what's your prediction for this season?
The division is marginally better, but the Patriots are still the Patriots. If Brady does miss four games they could start 1-3, but you know he'll be as motivated as ever to make it back to the playoffs. The big question, to me, is in the secondary. Losing Revis really hurts. He's a defensive game-changer more than you realize, and his replacement (Bradley Fletcher?) will need more safety help than Revis ever did. Looking ahead to the playoffs, can this team hold off Luck, Big Ben, and Flacco? I'm not sure I see it. Ten wins might be a stretch, but I see a focused Pats team making it back to the playoffs and falling just short of the Super Bowl.

The Pro Football Beast Prediction: **10-6**

Your Genius Prediction: _____

Predictions from Kickstarter Super Fans...

Aaron Motta | Tampa Bay, FL - Brady wants #5, and he'll make it back to the Super Bowl and beat the Packers in a shoot out, 35-31.

Nate DaCosta | Columbia, PA - The Patriots are good. They are better than the other teams. Tom Brady is good. He is better than the other quarterbacks.

BUFFALO BILLS

'14: 9-7 | 2nd AFC East | Missed Playoffs

WK 1	IND	2015 SCHED	
WK 2	NE	WK 10	@nyj
WK 3	@mia	WK 11	@ne
WK 4	NYG	WK 12	@kc
WK 5	@ten	WK 13	HOU
WK 6	CIN	WK 14	@phl
WK 7	@jax*	WK 15	@was
WK 8	BYE	WK 16	DAL
WK 9	MIA	WK 17	NYJ

Claim to Fame: The 54.0 sacks their defense racked up in 2014 led the league.

Team Anagram to represent last season:
Iso Bluff Ball

LOOKING AHEAD TO 2015...

Key Additions: LeSean McCoy (PHL), Matt Cassell (MIN), Percy Harvin (NYJ), Charles Clay (MIA), Ronald Darby (draft)
Key Subtractions: CJ Spiller (NO), Kiko Alonso (PHL), Da'Norris Searcy (TEN)
Key Multiplication: 4 x 8 = 32
Key Division: 39% of their fans love the hiring of Rex Ryan, the other 61% will get back to us when they're done shoveling snow from last winter some time in late September.

(HC) Rex Ryan, 1st yr | **(DC)** Dennis Thurman, 1st yr | **(OC)** Greg Roman, 1st yr
Base Defense: 3-4

EVERYTHING ELSE YOU NEED TO KNOW...

Do they play in London this year?
Yes. A Week 7 road game "at Jacksonville" at 9:30am ET on Oct. 25.

Do they play in Toronto this year?
Nope. The Bills played one home game per year there from 2008-2013, but never again.

How many prime time games are they scheduled for?
Two, including back to back division road games in November.

Do you have any other thoughts on their schedule?
Based on last year's records it's the 14th easiest in the league, but they should miss Tom Brady in Week 2....they open (and close) the season with two home games, but opening against both AFC Championship teams is hardly a good break...somehow they only have two home games between Halloween and Christmas, an abundant stretch of road games that you rarely see in the NFL.

EVERYTHING ELSE YOU NEED TO KNOW (CONT'D)...

What is their best-case and worst-case scenario for the season?
Best case, they go 16-0 and win the Super Bowl. Worst case, the entire northern half of New York realizes there are warmer places to live in the U.S. and the ensuing mass exodus to Florida starts another Civil War, ending life as we know it.

Can we play a fantasy football version of two lies and a truth?
Sure. One of these points might help you win your fantasy league, two definitely won't.

1. "Percy Harvin & The Olympians" is a great moniker for your fantasy team if you like to incorporate book titles, players, and ampersands into your team name.

2. Taking the Bills as your DEF is fine, just draft a backup for their Week 1 tilt against Indy and their Week 2 matchup against Tom Brady (if his suspension is lifted).

3. Bills' CB Rod Sweeting has the same birthday as me, but you shouldn't draft him as your starting running back just based on that because he's not a running back, he's a cornerback.

Is there anything about this team I don't know that I probably should?
RB LeSean McCoy's social security number is 023-47-6921.

Enough nonsense, what's your prediction for this season?
It was the best of times, it was the worst of times. (It was the Bills' offense, it was the Bills' defense.) The Bills' defensive front seven is the class of the AFC, and even with the switch to a Rex Ryan 3-4, they'll remain dominant. The problems lie in the offensive huddle, particularly at QB. Matt Cassell wasn't the answer in Minnesota, and he won't be the answer here. EJ Manuel wasn't the answer in Buffalo last year, and he still won't be the answer here. Who's left to try and run Greg Roman's complicated offensive scheme? Tyrod Taylor? Color me skeptical. Shady McCoy and Percy Harvin can be great weapons, but without a skilled leader at QB you're going to see a lot of 20-17 games. The talent on this roster is playoff-caliber, but without the right guy under center, it's more mediocrity in Orchard Park.

The Pro Football Beast Prediction: **8-8**

Your Genius Prediction: _____

MIAMI DOLPHINS

'14: 8-8 | 3rd AFC East | Missed Playoffs

WK1	@was	2015 SCHED	
WK 2	@jax	WK 10	@phl
WK 3	BUF	WK 11	DAL
WK 4	NYJ*	WK 12	@nyj
WK 5	BYE	WK 13	BAL
WK 6	@ten	WK 14	NYG
WK 7	HOU	WK 15	@sd
WK 8	@ne	WK 16	IND
WK 9	@buf	WK 17	NE

Claim to Fame: No QB has been sacked more than Ryan Tannehill (139) since 2012.

Team Anagram to represent last season: Old Mini Mishap

LOOKING AHEAD TO 2015...

Key Additions: Ndamukong Suh (DET), Kenny Stills (NO), Jordan Cameron (CLE), Greg Jennings (MIN), DeVante Parker (draft)
Key Subtractions: Mike Wallace (MIN), Charles Clay (BUF), Jared Odrick (JAX), Brian Hartline (CLE), Phillip Wheeler (SF)
Key Multiplication: 7 x 2 = 14
Key Division: 39% of their players have heard of the TV show Flipper, the other 61% were born in the mid-90s and wow, do we feel old right about now.

(HC) Joe Philbin, 4th yr | **(DC)** Kevin Coyle, 4th yr | **(OC)** Bill Lazor, 2nd yr
Base Defense: 4-3

EVERYTHING ELSE YOU NEED TO KNOW...

Do they play in London this year?
Yes. A Week 4 "home game" vs. the NY Jets at 9:30am ET on Oct. 4.

Do they play in Madrid this year?
Nope. The NFL does not play games there, you payaso.

How many prime time games are they scheduled for?
Two, including at New England on the last Thursday in October on short rest.

Do you have any other thoughts on their schedule?
Based on last year's records it's the 16th easiest in the league....they play seven of nine on the road to start the season thanks to a "home" game in London...but four of their last five are at home, and the only road game is in San Diego, so it will be a warm holiday season for the fins and their fans...closing the season against both AFC Championship could be a tough draw if playoff spots and seeding are in play...the Dolphins will be wearing throwback uniforms during their Week 14 game against the Giants.

EVERYTHING ELSE YOU NEED TO KNOW (CONT'D)...

What is their best-case and worst-case scenario for the season?
Best case, they go 16-0 and win the Super Bowl. Worst case, Joe Philbin's less-than-vibrant personality implodes on itself like an inverted supernova during the first quarter of their opener, creating the largest black hole the world has ever seen that sucks in the entire universe, ending life as we know it.

Can we play a fantasy football version of two lies and a truth?
How about we just go with one truth for the Dolphins?

1. If you're strategy is to be the last guy to draft a QB, you should still be able to land Brady, Romo, or Ryan Tannehill in Rounds 9 or 10 of a 10-team league. And of those three, only Tannehill posted double-digit fantasy points in 15 of 16 games in 2014. He's not a sexy name, but in Bill Lazor's system he delivers.

Is there anything about this team I don't know that I probably should?
The dolphin in Miami's logo is named Heather McDumps.

Enough nonsense, what's your prediction for this season?
Many are picking the Dolphins as a favorite for one of the two AFC wild card slots, I'm just not sure I'm there yet. Ryan Tannehill thrived under Bill Lazor's new scheme in 2014, but four of their top five receivers from last year are gone. Are DeVante Parker and Kenny Stills an upgrade to their WR core? Maybe, but they'll have to learn the system and develop chemistry with Tannehill quickly. The addition of Suh bolsters a defense that was 24th against the rush last year, but there are still question marks at LB and in the secondary. They'll need a good start because their final five games down the stretch could all be difficult. Maybe it's a lack of confidence in Joe Philbin, but I see this team improving by only one win, just missing the playoffs.

The Pro Football Beast Prediction: **9-7**

Your Genius Prediction: _____

Predictions from Kickstarter Super Fans...

Shawn Erb | Tampa Bay, FL - After 15 long years, we finally have a QB worth building around. They're committed to Tannehill and he'll continue to improve. Suh fixes the issues on D, so I expect them to challenge for the AFC East title. PREDICTION: 10-6

NEW YORK JETS

'14: 4-12 | 4th AFC East | Missed Playoffs

WK 1	CLE	2015 SCHED	
WK 2	@ind	WK 10	BUF
WK 3	PHL	WK 11	@hou
WK 4	@mia*	WK 12	MIA
WK 5	BYE	WK 13	@nyg
WK 6	WAS	WK 14	TEN
WK 7	@ne	WK 15	@dal
WK 8	@oak	WK 16	NE
WK 9	JAX	WK 17	@buf

Claim to Fame: They tallied 181.4 passing yards/game in 2014, fewest in the NFL.

Team Anagram to represent last season:
Jerks, Ye Won't

LOOKING AHEAD TO 2015...

Key Additions: Brandon Marshall (CHI), Darrelle Revis (NE), Ryan Fitzpatrick (HOU), Antonio Cromartie (ARI), Buster Skrine (CLE), Zac Stacy (STL), Stevan Ridley (NE), Leonard Williams (draft)
Key Subtractions: Percy Harvin (BUF), Kyle Wilson (NO), Kenrick Ellis (NYG)
Key Multiplication: 1 x 18 = 18
Key Division: 39% of New Yorkers cheer for the Giants, the other 61% hate-watch the Jets and call it fandom.

(HC) Todd Bowles, 1st yr | **(DC)** Kacy Rodgers, 1st yr | **(OC)** Chan Gailey, 1st yr
Base Defense: 3-4

EVERYTHING ELSE YOU NEED TO KNOW...

Do they play in London this year?
Yes. A Week 4 road game "at Miami" at 9:30am ET on Oct. 4.

Do they play in Cape Town this year?
Nope. The NFL does not play games there, you loser.

How many prime time games are they scheduled for?
Three, including a Saturday night game at Dallas on December 19th.

Do you have any other thoughts on their schedule?
Based on last year's records it's the 15th easiest in the league....having the Colts and Eagles in September will put Todd Bowles' new defense to the test right away...their Week 13 road game at the Giants features a fairly short commute...finishing against the Cowboys, Patriots, and Bills will be a tough task if the Jets are still in playoff contention...unfortunately for them, they won't play the Pats while Brady is suspended.

EVERYTHING ELSE YOU NEED TO KNOW (CONT'D)...

What is their best-case and worst-case scenario for the season?
Best case, they go 16-0 and win the Super Bowl. Worst case, they go 16-0, make it to the Super Bowl, and hours before the game Armageddon begins, ending life as we know it.

Can we play a fantasy football version of two lies and a truth?
Sure. One of these points might help you win your fantasy league, two definitely won't.

1. When RB Chris Ivory gets drafted yell out, "Chris Ebony and Ivory Soap!" as if that's his nickname, because let's be honest, it should be.

2. Just for fun, draft a real player no one as ever heard of with your last pick. Quincy Enunwa, for example, is a second-year WR from Nebraska. Go ahead, take him!

3. Brandon Marshall is an interesting case this year. He's an elite WR, but the Jets' roster is where receivers go to die, which is why he's not being drafted until the 7th round. I think he's a solid option at WR3, and if you can grab him with your 7th pick, you should.

Is there anything about this team I don't know that I probably should?
New head coach Todd Bowles likes to place large orders in fast-food drive-thrus and then drive off, just to create employee chaos. He thinks it's hilarious, but it's not, Todd. It's not.

Enough nonsense, what's your prediction for this season?
There are almost enough similarities between this Jets team and the Bills that I was tempted to start this paragraph by copy and pasting Buffalo's writeup. A strong defense, a new coaching staff, and major questions at QB are the headlines for both. Looking deeper, however, reveals a Jets team still in need of an identity. They were third in the league in rushing last year, but new O.C. Chan Gailey is implementing a new scheme that could set the running game back. The hope is that his spread offense will bring the most out of Geno Smith, but some wonder if his ceiling is high enough to be a successful starting QB, even with a new toy like Brandon Marshall. The defense should be among the league's best with the return of Revis and Cromartie to the secondary, and rookie Leonard Williams will bolster an already good defensive line. I see this as a transition year for the Jets, as Todd Bowles works through his learning curve and figures out who his guys are. The pieces are there, and this year could be a small step in the direction of getting this team back to the playoffs in 2016.

The Pro Football Beast Prediction: **7-9**

Your Genius Prediction: _____

PITTSBURGH STEELERS

'14: 11-5 | 1st AFC North | #4 AFC Seed

		2015 SCHED	
WK 1	@ne		
WK 2	SF	WK 10	CLE
WK 3	@stl	WK 11	BYE
WK 4	BAL	WK 12	@sea
WK 5	@sd	WK 13	IND
WK 6	ARI	WK 14	@cin
WK 7	@kc	WK 15	DEN
WK 8	CIN	WK 16	@bal
WK 9	OAK	WK 17	@cle

Claim to Fame: No AFC offense averaged a higher time of possession last year (32:24).

Team Anagram to represent last season:
Slightest Burp Reset

LOOKING AHEAD TO 2015...

Key Additions: DeAngelo Williams (CAR), Bud Dupree (draft)
Key Subtractions: Jason Worilds (retired), Troy Polamalu (retired), Brice McCain (MIA)
Key Multiplication: 2 x 1000 = 2000
Key Division: 39% of their team said the locker room presence they'd miss most this year is Troy Polamalu, the other 61% said Troy Polamalu's hair.

(HC) Mike Tomlin, 9th yr | **(DC)** Keith Butler, 1st yr | **(OC)** Todd Haley, 4th yr
Base Defense: 3-4

EVERYTHING ELSE YOU NEED TO KNOW...

Do they play in London this year?
Nope. They lost to the Vikings in London in 2013, 34-27.

Do they play at Augusta National this year?
Nope. That's a golf course.

How many prime time games are they scheduled for?
Five, including the season opener at New England.

Do you have any other thoughts on their schedule?
Based on last year's records it's the #1 toughest in the league...they open the season against the champs (huge break: no Tom Brady)...they have nine games against playoff teams from last year...they have the Ravens on short rest after a road game...plus they close the season with a difficult six game stretch against 3 division rivals, Seattle, Denver, and Indy...again, HUGE break not facing Brady in Week 1 thanks to his suspension (if it is upheld)...they will wear throwback uniforms in Week 8 against the Bengals.

EVERYTHING ELSE YOU NEED TO KNOW (CONT'D)...

What is their best-case and worst-case scenario for the season?
Best case, they go 16-0 and win the Super Bowl. Worst case, the Heinz factory has a code red meltdown flooding the entire city in a sea of ketchup that accelerates global warming and causes solar flares to scorch the entire solar system, ending life as we know it.

Can we play a fantasy football version of two lies and a truth?
Sure. One of these points might help you win your fantasy league, two definitely won't.

1. If you have a Steelers fan in your league, they will undoubtedly wear their Steelers jersey to the draft just to annoy you. There's a 91% chance it's "Bettis" or "Polamalu."

2. His name is Martavis Bryant, not Martavius Bryant. If the owner in your league who drafts him says his name incorrectly ("MAR-TAY-VEE-US"), he has not drafted Martavis Bryant, he has drafted someone who doesn't exist. With your last pick draft "MAR-TAY-VIS Bryant" and explain why he was still available. You will be hated, and possibly kicked out of the league, but all is fair in love and war and fantasy football.

3. Don't touch the Steelers' DEF this year. They're not great and they play a lot of solid offenses. The only exception would be if you want to stream them in weeks 9 & 10, and then drop them for better match-ups.

Is there anything about this team I don't know that I probably should?
TE Heath Miller knows it won't burn him, but he is still scared to touch aluminum foil that has been in the oven. His brain just can't grasp the concept that it won't feel hot.

Enough nonsense, what's your prediction for this season?
These are the Steelers in a mirror. Everything is backwards. The defense? Not great, especially in the secondary. Dick LeBeau is gone, and while Keith Butler will provide continuity from last year, expect some growing pains as the unit adjusts to a new chief. The offense, on the other hand, remains dynamic. The only team last year to average over 300 passing yds/gm and over 105 rushing yds/gm can beat you in the air and on the ground. They will be in a lot of shootouts this year, and despite playing an insanely tough schedule, they'll win a couple more than they lose. Big Ben will emerge as a legit MVP candidate and Mike Tomlin, with his new 2-year contract, will return the post-season once again with a Week 17 win over the Browns.

The Pro Football Beast Prediction: **9-7**

Your Genius Prediction: _____

CINCINNATI BENGALS

'14: 10-5-1 | 2nd AFC North | #5 AFC Seed

WK1	@oak	2015 SCHED	
WK 2	SD	WK 10	HOU
WK 3	@bal	WK 11	@ari
WK 4	KC	WK 12	STL
WK 5	SEA	WK 13	@cle
WK 6	@buf	WK 14	PIT
WK 7	BYE	WK 15	@sf
WK 8	@pit	WK 16	@den
WK 9	CLE	WK 17	BAL

Claim to Fame: Their defense had 20 sacks last season, fewest in the NFL.

Team Anagram to represent last season: Enticing Cannibals

LOOKING AHEAD TO 2015...

Key Additions: Pat Sims (OAK), Michael Johnson (TB), Denarius Moore (OAK), A.J. Hawk (GB), Cedric Ogbuehi (draft)
Key Subtractions: Jermaine Gresham (ARI), Marshall Newhouse (NYG)
Key Multiplication: -5 x -5 = 25
Key Division: 39% of their fans are happy that Marvin Lewis just signed another contract extension, the other 61% actually want to win in the playoffs.

(HC) Marvin Lewis, 13th yr | **(DC)** Paul Guenther, 2nd yr | **(OC)** Hue Jackson, 2nd yr
Base Defense: 4-3

EVERYTHING ELSE YOU NEED TO KNOW...

Do they play in London this year?
Nope. Never have, either.

Do they play in Nairobi this year?
Nope. The NFL does not play games there, you fail hashtag.

How many prime time games are they scheduled for?
Four, including two sets of back-to-backs (Weeks 9/10 and 15/16).

Do you have any other thoughts on their schedule?
Based on last year's records it's the 2nd toughest in the league....they start on the road for the sixth straight year...they have four prime time games but are only 3-11 in those regular season night games since 2008...five of their last ten games are division games...road night games at San Francisco and Denver in Weeks 15 and 16 might make it tough to make up ground in the standings late in the year.

EVERYTHING ELSE YOU NEED TO KNOW (CONT'D)...

What is their best-case and worst-case scenario for the season?
Best case, they go 16-0 and win the Super Bowl. Worst case, they go 16-0 but they lose their first playoff game 63-0 with Andy Dalton going 0-37 with 13 interceptions. Following the game their fans storm the locker room with pitchforks and torches, and the ensuing riot leads to World War III, ending life as we know it.

Can we play a fantasy football version of two lies and a truth?
Sure. One of these points might help you win your fantasy league, two definitely won't.

1. A.J. Green has suffered a concussion in one consecutive night game against Pittsburgh. Good news for this year, since both Steeler games are during the day.

2. Bring a lemon meringue pie to your draft and tell everyone, "this is the Gio Bernard pie." When somebody drafts him, get out of your seat, smash the pie in their face, and sit back down without saying a word.

3. Are you comfortable with Jeremy Hill as your RB1? You should be. If you've got one of the last picks in the first round, grab him and feel great about it.

Is there anything about this team I don't know that I probably should?
WR Mohamed Sanu can only fall asleep to simulated womb noises.

Enough nonsense, what's your prediction for this season?
Will the only team in league history to go one-and-done in the playoffs four straight years make it back? I'm not betting on it. I think we've seen the best that Marvin Lewis and Andy Dalton have to offer, and under the bright lights of the big games, it leaves much to be desired. Depth and injury issues on defense could slow down an already mediocre roster, and if they're not able to manufacture turnovers like they did last year (20 INTs ranked 3rd in the NFL), they could be playing from behind more than they want. With Jeremy Hill and A.J. Green healthy they remain a quick strike offense capable of erasing deficits in a hurry, but I see regression to the pack in the AFC North. Call it a hunch, or call it not wanting to see the Bengals play any more terrible playoff games, but I have them missing the post-season this year with a .500 record.

The Pro Football Beast Prediction: **8-8**

Your Genius Prediction: _____

BALTIMORE RAVENS

'14: 10-6 | 3rd AFC North | #6 AFC Seed

WK1	@den	2015 SCHED	
WK 2	@oak	WK 10	JAX
WK 3	CIN	WK 11	STL
WK 4	@pit	WK 12	@cle
WK 5	CLE	WK 13	@mia
WK 6	@sf	WK 14	SEA
WK 7	@ari	WK 15	KC
WK 8	SD	WK 16	PIT
WK 9	BYE	WK 17	@cin

Claim to Fame: Their defense only had 22 takeaways in 2014, tied for fewest in their history.

Team Anagram to represent last season: Rant is Removable

LOOKING AHEAD TO 2015...

Key Additions: Matt Schaub (HOU), Kendrick Lewis (HOU), Aldrick Robinson (WAS), Breshad Perriman (draft)
Key Subtractions: Haloti Ngata (DET), Pernell McPhee (CHI), Torrey Smith (SF), Owen Daniels (DEN), Darian Stewart (DEN), Jacoby Jones (SD)
Key Multiplication: 365 x 1 = 365
Key Division: 39% of their team thinks Roger Goodell mishandled the Ray Rice situation last year, the other 61% replaced 'mishandled' with 'took a hot dump on.'

(HC) John Harbaugh, 8th yr | **(DC)** Dean Pees, 4th yr | **(OC)** Marc Trestman, 1st yr
Base Defense: 3-4

EVERYTHING ELSE YOU NEED TO KNOW...

Do they play in London this year?
Nope. Never have, either.

Do they play in the core of the earth this year?
Nope. The core of the earth is 10,800 degrees Fahrenheit.

How many prime time games are they scheduled for?
Five, including both games against the Steelers.

Do you have any other thoughts on their schedule?
Based on last year's records it's the 11th toughest in the league....they open the season with long trips to Denver and Oakland...their only road game in November comes on the last day of the month...both of their Monday Night games are on the road...they finish the season with the Steelers and Bengals, in what will likely be a close division race.

EVERYTHING ELSE YOU NEED TO KNOW (CONT'D)...

What is their best-case and worst-case scenario for the season?
Best case, they go 16-0 and win the Super Bowl. Worst case, Joe Flacco changes his name to 'Elite Joe Flacco' and tells reporters that *The Wire* is the worst television show he's ever seen. Television enthusiasts all over the world lose their minds and start World War III, ending life as we know it.

Can we play a fantasy football version of two lies and a truth?
Sure. One of these points might help you win your fantasy league, two definitely won't.

1. The Ravens will be wearing their Edgar Allen Poe throwback uniforms against the Chargers in Week 8, which feature actual raven feathers sewn into the fabric. Expect big games out of all their offensive players because no one wants to touch real bird feathers.

2. Everyone loves drafting a high upside rookie, but don't reach too far for WR Breshad Perriman. If he's there in Round 12, go for it, but guys like Brian Quick, Davante Adams, and even Marques Colston might give you similar numbers from Rounds 13 or 14.

3. Rumors are swirling in Baltimore that kicker Justin Tucker might protest the new extra point rule by kicking them with his left foot. Stay away on draft day.

Is there anything about this team I don't know that I probably should?
HC John Harbaugh's first job in the NFL was unwrapping Halls' vitamin C drops for Eagles coach Ray Rhodes, picking out all the grapefruit drops, and placing them in Ray's mouth whenever he coughed, cleared his throat, or said the word 'tackle'.

Enough nonsense, what's your prediction for this season?
The biggest change for the Ravens coming into this season is the switch at Offensive Coordinator. Marc Trestman will be looking to remind everyone why he was touted as an offensive genius coming into the league by opening up the passing game more. Breshad Perriman and Maxx Williams, their two top draft picks, should help the cause. Their defense remains above average thanks to the brilliant edge rushing of thirty-somethings Elvis Dumervil and Terrell Suggs and the standout linebacking play of 23-year old C.J. Mosley. It's a schedule front-loaded with road games, so getting to their Week 9 bye with five wins would be huge. I think they will, and I think they win the division.

The Pro Football Beast Prediction: **10-6**

Your Genius Prediction: _____

CLEVELAND BROWNS

'14: 7-9 | 4th AFC North | Missed Playoffs

		2015 SCHED	
WK 1	@nyj		
WK 2	TEN	WK 10	@pit
WK 3	OAK	WK 11	BYE
WK 4	@sd	WK 12	BAL
WK 5	@bal	WK 13	CIN
WK 6	DEN	WK 14	SF
WK 7	@stl	WK 15	@sea
WK 8	ARI	WK 16	@kc
WK 9	@cin	WK 17	PIT

Claim to Fame: At 29.5%, they had the worst 3rd down conversion rate in the NFL in 2014.

Team Anagram to represent last season:
Verbal Clown Dens

LOOKING AHEAD TO 2015...

Key Additions: Tramon Williams (GB), Brian Hartline (MIA), Josh McCown (TB), Danny Shelton (draft)
Key Subtractions: Jordan Cameron (MIA), Jabaal Sheard (NE), Buster Skrine (NYJ), Brian Hoyer (HOU)
Key Multiplication: 4 x 44 = 176
Key Division: 39% of their fans are excited about the uniform rebrand, the other 61% won't even notice it until November.

(HC) Mike Pettine, 2nd yr | **(DC)** Jim O'Neil, 2nd yr | **(OC)** John DeFilippo, 1st yr
Base Defense: 3-4

EVERYTHING ELSE YOU NEED TO KNOW...

Do they play in London this year?
Nope. Never have, either.

Do they play on Kepler 452b this year?
Nope. The NFL does not play games there, Neil Armstrong.

How many prime time games are they scheduled for?
Two, and both are division games.

Do you have any other thoughts on their schedule?
Based on last year's records it's the 9th toughest in the league....they open the season against the three worst teams on their schedule (at NYJ, vs. TEN, vs. OAK)...they play four division games in a row (Weeks 9 through 13)...they only have two road games after Thanksgiving, but they are in the two loudest stadiums in the league (SEA/KC).

EVERYTHING ELSE YOU NEED TO KNOW (CONT'D)...

What is their best-case and worst-case scenario for the season?
Best case, they go 16-0 and win the Super Bowl. Worst case, LeBron James is on the sidelines watching their home opener in Week 2 when Johnny Manziel runs him over with a golf cart, ending his basketball career, and causing their fans start World War III, ending life as we know it.

Can we play a fantasy football version of two lies and a truth?
Sure. One of these points might help you win your fantasy league, two definitely won't.

1. I ran into WR Brian Hartline in an elevator last month and asked him how he's feeling about this year. "Great," he said. Based on that, make him the first WR you select.

2. Imagine winning your league with Johnny Manziel on your roster all year? I dare you to draft him with your last pick, rename your team "Johnny Benchwarmer", stash him on your bench all year, and still win your league. Seriously, try it.

3. If you like to stream defenses (changing them week depending on the matchup), consider starting with the Browns. They open with the Jets, Titans, and Raiders, so you might be able to draft them in the last round and get solid points in the first few weeks.

Is there anything about this team I don't know that I probably should?
They have the worst team name in any sport in any league in any country in any solar system in any galaxy in the universe. (But maybe you already knew that.)

Enough nonsense, what's your prediction for this season?
The only team to win fewer games over the last 5 years than the Browns (25) is the Jaguars (22). If you're scoring at home, that's not good company. Yes, they finished 7-9 last year, but that included a dreadful 0-5 finish. On offense the only bright spot is their offensive line. It's a train wreck everywhere else, including what could be the worst wide receiver group in the entire league. Any hope that Cleveland fans have this year has to be pinned on the defense, which features one of the league's best secondaries. That being said, no team gave up more rushing yards last year than the Browns, an issue they tried to address with draft picks Danny Shelton and Nate Orchard. I'd like to think they can ground and pound their way to seven wins again, but a tough schedule and a shaky QB situation don't give me much hope. For the Dawg Pound's sake, I hope I'm wrong.

The Pro Football Beast Prediction: **4-12**

Your Genius Prediction: _____

INDIANAPOLIS COLTS

'14: 11-5 | 1st AFC South | #3 AFC Seed

WK 1	@buf	2015 SCHED	
WK 2	NYJ	WK 10	BYE
WK 3	@ten	WK 11	@atl
WK 4	JAX	WK 12	TB
WK 5	@hou	WK 13	@pit
WK 6	NE	WK 14	@jax
WK 7	NO	WK 15	HOU
WK 8	@car	WK 16	@mia
WK 9	DEN	WK 17	TEN

Claim to Fame: They have finished 11-5 in all three of Andrew Luck's years in the league.

Team Anagram to represent last season: Spinal Dislocation

LOOKING AHEAD TO 2015...

Key Additions: Frank Gore (SF), Andre Johnson (HOU), Trent Cole (PHL), Phillip Dorsett (draft)
Key Subtractions: Hakeem Nicks (TEN), Josh Gordy (NYG), Ricky Jean Francois (WAS)
Key Multiplication: 4 x 38 = 152
Key Division: 39% of their fans think Andrew Luck should run this team for the next eight years, 61% think Andrew Luck should run the country for the next eight years.

(HC) Chuck Pagano, 4th yr | **(DC)** Greg Manusky, 4th yr | **(OC)** Pep Hamilton, 3rd yr
Base Defense: 3-4

EVERYTHING ELSE YOU NEED TO KNOW...

Do they play in London this year?
Nope. Never have, either.

Do they play in Ho Chi Minh City this year?
Nope. The NFL does not play games there, you piece of filth.

How many prime time games are they scheduled for?
Five, including an AFC Championship game rematch hosting NE in Week 6.

Do you have any other thoughts on their schedule?
Based on last year's records it's the 2nd easiest in the league, thanks to how terrible the rest of this division is....they get the Patriots and the Broncos at home, though that New England game looks like it will be Tom Brady's return from suspension...their only road game coming off a road game is at JAX...no team has a better chance to start 5-0 the way their schedule lines up...their only chance for a cold-weather game is week 13 at PIT.

EVERYTHING ELSE YOU NEED TO KNOW (CONT'D)...

What is their best-case and worst-case scenario for the season?
Best case, they go 16-0 and win the Super Bowl. Worst case, the pitch of Andrew Luck's voice gets even lower, and an audible he calls out in Week 6 creates a fault line under the Mississippi River that swallows up the entire continent, ending life as we know it.

Can we play a fantasy football version of two lies and a truth?
Sure. One of these points might help you win your fantasy league, two definitely won't.

1. Want to make a bold statement in your draft this year? Go all Colts with your first 10 picks: Luck, Hilton, Gore, Johnson, Moncrief, Allen, Herron, Fleener, Vinatieri, and the Colts DEF. I guarantee you'll be the highlight of the draft, even if your team sucks.

2. RB Vick Ballard claims to have graduated from Mississippi State, but no one has ever seen his actual diploma. Can you trust a guy like that on your team? I don't think so.

3. If you're the kind of owner who loves looking smart for taking a flier late in the draft, consider rookie WR Phillip Dorsett. He's fourth on the Indy depth chart, but he's drawing early rave reviews. If your league is deep enough, he might be worth a bench spot.

Is there anything about this team I don't know that I probably should?
TE Duane Allen has never had PMS.

Enough nonsense, what's your prediction for this season?
What's not to like about this team? Very little. Andrew Luck has gone 11-5 in all three of his seasons, and this year's schedule is another piece of cake thanks to their craptastic division. Luck has more weapons on offense, though one wonders if the upgrades should have been made to the offensive line, especially since the Colts cut Gosder Cherilus in late July. The defense remains mediocre as a whole, but playing with a lead covers a multitude of sins. With the Patriots potentially Brady-less for 4 games, the Broncos looking vulnerable, and the bloodbath that is the AFC North, the window is now for the Colts to get 12 or more wins and secure home field advantage for the playoffs. I think they'll do it, and I like their chances of hosting the AFC Championship game on January 24th, 2016. Can Luck win the big one? Of course he can. Will he get there? That might be THE question of 2015.

The Pro Football Beast Prediction: **13-3**

Your Genius Prediction: _____

HOUSTON TEXANS

'14: 9-7 | 2nd AFC North | Missed Playoffs

WK 1	KC	2015 SCHED	
WK 2	@car	WK 10	@cin
WK 3	TB	WK 11	NYJ
WK 4	@atl	WK 12	NO
WK 5	IND	WK 13	@buf
WK 6	@jax	WK 14	NE
WK 7	@mia	WK 15	@ind
WK 8	TEN	WK 16	@ten
WK 9	BYE	WK 17	JAX

Claim to Fame: They ran the ball on 51.9% of plays last year, the most in the NFL.

Team Anagram to represent last season:
Snot Nut Hoaxes

LOOKING AHEAD TO 2015...

Key Additions: Vince Wilfork (NE), Rahim Moore (DEN), Cecil Shorts (JAX), Brian Hoyer (CLE), Kevin Johnson (draft)
Key Subtractions: Brooks Reed (ATL), Andre Johnson (IND), D.J. Swearinger (TB)
Key Multiplication: 99 x 1 = 99
Key Division: 39% of their roster weight comes from 52.5 guys, the other 61% comes from the left side of Vince Wilfork's body.

(HC) Bill O'Brien, 2nd yr | **(DC)** Romeo Crennel, 2nd yr | **(OC)** George Godsey, 1st yr
Base Defense: 3-4

EVERYTHING ELSE YOU NEED TO KNOW...

Do they play in London this year?
Nope. Never have, either.

Do they play in London this year?
Nope. You literally just asked me that.

How many prime time games are they scheduled for?
Two, including hosting the Colts on three days of rest on a Thursday in Week 5.

Do you have any other thoughts on their schedule?
Based on last year's records it's the 3rd easiest in the league...they open and close the season at home...they get the Bengals in prime time, which is usually bad for the Bengals...December probably stacks up as their toughest month with three road games and a lone home game against the defending champion Patriots.

EVERYTHING ELSE YOU NEED TO KNOW (CONT'D)...

What is their best-case and worst-case scenario for the season?
Best case, they go 16-0 and win the Super Bowl. Worst case, the Texans start off 7-0 and look unbeatable, but the Astros finally win their first world series by sweeping the Cubs and the ensuing fracas spills over into Mexico causing the destruction of the U.S.-Mexican border, leading to World War III and ending life as we know it.

Can we play a fantasy football version of two lies and a truth?
Sure. One of these points might help you win your fantasy league, two definitely won't.

1. WR DeAndre Hopkins averaged 127 yds/gm when he ate eggs for breakfast and only 39 yds/gm when he ate cereal. Break into his hotel room this year to find out what he's eating and illegally stalk your way to fantasy glory.

2. Never draft a player born on Halloween. I'm looking at you, rookie RB Kenny Hilliard.

3. WR DeAndre Hopkins is being drafted in the top of the fifth round as a WR2, but I think that's a bit of a stretch. I'd rather have Jordan Matthews, Julian Edelman, or Brandin Cooks, all guys who are being taken after him.

Is there anything about this team I don't know that I probably should?
For the past decade, the Texans' grounds crew have a tradition of urinating on the field in the North End Zone the night before each game. It's kind of gross.

Enough nonsense, what's your prediction for this season?
The fact that training camp started in Houston with a true competition at QB tells you all you need to know about their offense: they don't have the answer yet. I expect Hoyer to beat out Mallett for the job, but either way they'll look to establish the run early and often while peppering in the passing game. (Note: Arian Foster's groin injury as this book went to press could put a damper on that.) Talk of their defense begins and ends with all-world J.J. Watt, but they will need better play from their secondary to make a playoff push this year. No team had more takeaways than Houston last year, and while some of that can be pinned on Watt's brilliance, turnover differential can be a volatile stat in the NFL from year to year. If a healthy Jadeveon Clowney and Brian Cushing can help the Titans split with the Colts this year, they've got a chance at the wild card, but in a QB-dominated league, I still see them on the outside looking in.

The Pro Football Beast Prediction: **8-8**

Your Genius Prediction: _____

JACKSONVILLE JAGUARS

'14: 3-13 | 3rd AFC South | Missed Playoffs

WK1	CAR	2015 SCHED	
WK 2	MIA	WK 10	@bal
WK 3	@ne	WK 11	TEN
WK 4	@ind	WK 12	SD
WK 5	@tb	WK 13	@ten
WK 6	HOU	WK 14	IND
WK 7	BUF*	WK 15	ATL
WK 8	BYE	WK 16	@no
WK 9	@nyj	WK 17	@hou

Claim to Fame: The last four seasons they are 14-50, worst in the NFL over that span.

Team Anagram to represent last season:
Jill Nova Suckage Jars

LOOKING AHEAD TO 2015...

Key Additions: Julius Thomas (DEN), Stefen Wisniewski (OAK), Jared Odrick (MIA), Jermey Parnell (DAL), Dante Fowler Jr. (draft)
Key Subtractions: Cecil Shorts (HOU), Jacques McClendon (MIA), J.T. Thomas (NYG)
Key Multiplication: 13 x 13 = 169
Key Division: 39% of Jaguars' fans think their two-tone helmets are hideous, the other 61% should have their eyes checked because they are an abomination.

(HC) Gus Bradley, 3rd yr | **(DC)** Bob Babich, 3rd yr | **(OC)** Greg Olson, 1st yr
Base Defense: 4-3

EVERYTHING ELSE YOU NEED TO KNOW...

Do they play in London this year?
Of course. A Week 7 "home game" vs. Buffalo at 9:30am ET on Oct. 25.

Do they play in Jacksonville this year?
Yes, that is their home city you donkey-brained sycophant.

How many prime time games are they scheduled for?
One, hosting the Titans on a Thursday in Week 11.

Do you have any other thoughts on their schedule?
Based on last year's records it's the 8th easiest in the league....all eight of their home games come in pairs on the schedule (though Week 7 is "home" in London)...they play both AFC Championship teams on the road in back to back weeks (Weeks 3 and 4)...their quest for a .500 season will finish up on the road in New Orleans and Houston.

EVERYTHING ELSE YOU NEED TO KNOW (CONT'D)...

What is their best-case and worst-case scenario for the season?
Best case, they go 16-0 and win the Super Bowl. Worst case, nothing changes.

Can we play a fantasy football version of two lies and a truth?
Sure. One of these points might help you win your fantasy league, two definitely won't.

1. Bored with fantasy? Try drafting an All-Monogram team featuring Blake Bortles and other players with the same two initials. Target Julio Jones, Steve Smith, Ameer Abdullah, Ray Rice (hoping he gets picked up), Eric Ebron, Marcus Mariota, Nick Novak, DEN Defense, and Eddie Lacy (hoping he changes his name to Larry).

2. Some folks are skittish about drafting Jacksonville's skill players, but there could be value there. Rookie RB T.J. Yeldon is going early in the 7th round and WR Allen Robinson is going late in the 9th, but I wouldn't mind taking them in the 6th and 8th, respectively.

3. In a Fantasy Coach league? Take Gus Bradley with your 1st pick. Also, get a job.

Is there anything about this team I don't know that I probably should?
The Jaguars' logo looks backwards in the mirror.

Enough nonsense, what's your prediction for this season?
On paper the Jaguars did everything they needed to do this off-season to overhaul their woeful offense. Blake Bortles worked on his mechanics with QB guru Tom House, Greg Olson was promoted to replace Jedd Fisch, T.J. Yeldon was drafted to improve the run game, and the O-line was upgraded through free agency, the draft, and with the hiring of Doug Marrone. Will it all matter? We'll see. The defense did not perform well last year, but it's tough to blame them when they were so rarely playing with a lead. Jared Odrick strengthens an already good defensive line, but on the whole it's a mediocre defense that could have really used Dante Fowler Jr., their first round pick who is out for the season after tearing an ACL in the first hour of rookie minicamp. No team scored fewer points per game last year than Jacksonville (15.6), but if their off-season changes bump that number up by even just two field goals, it could lead to five or six wins. I think it will, and while they won't hit .500, they are finally headed in the right direction.

The Pro Football Beast Prediction: **5-11**

Your Genius Prediction: _____

TENNESSEE TITANS

'14: 2-14 | 4th AFC North | Missed Playoffs

WK1	@tb	2015 SCHED	
WK 2	@cle	WK 10	CAR
WK 3	IND	WK 11	@jax
WK 4	BYE	WK 12	OAK
WK 5	BUF	WK 13	JAX
WK 6	MIA	WK 14	@nyj
WK 7	ATL	WK 15	@ne
WK 8	@hou	WK 16	HOU
WK 9	@no	WK 17	@ind

Claim to Fame: Their defense only had 731 penalty yards last season, fewest in the AFC.

Team Anagram to represent last season:
Insane Testes Net

LOOKING AHEAD TO 2015...

Key Additions: Brian Orakpo (WAS), Da'Norris Searcy (BUF), Hakeem Nicks (IND), Perrish Cox (SF), Marcus Mariota (draft)
Key Subtractions: Jake Locker (retired), Bernard Pollard (FA), Shonn Greene (FA)
Key Multiplication: 26 x 1 = 26
Key Division: 39% of their locker room cried during the first ten minutes of a screening of Pixar's *Up*, the other 61% are liars.

(HC) Ken Whisenhunt, 2nd yr | **(DC)** Ray Horton, 2nd yr | **(OC)** Jason Michael, 2nd yr
Base Defense: 3-4

EVERYTHING ELSE YOU NEED TO KNOW...

Do they play in London this year?
Nope. Never have, either.

Do they play in Qatar this year?
Nope. Unlike FIFA, the NFL has not yet been paid off to play games there.

How many prime time games are they scheduled for?
One, a Week 11 game in Jacksonville that no one will watch.

Do you have any other thoughts on their schedule?
Based on last year's records it's the 7th easiest in the league....Mariota vs. Winston in Week 1 will be fun...they open and close on the road, but they never have to travel farther west than Houston...14 of their 16 games are scheduled for 1pm Eastern starts...they have no away games in October, going six weeks between road tilts...it's a tough finish, with road games against both AFC Championship teams in the last three weeks of the season.

EVERYTHING ELSE YOU NEED TO KNOW (CONT'D)...

What is their best-case and worst-case scenario for the season?
Best case, they go 16-0 and win the Super Bowl. Worst case, Marcus Mariota does a cameo on the ABC show *Nashville* and during the last take a lighting rig falls directly on his right hand, severing off three fingers and a thumb. He quits football to take up acting, and their fans start World War III, ending life as we know it.

Can we play a fantasy football version of two lies and a truth?
Sure. One of these points might help you win your fantasy league, two definitely won't.

1. When it's time to grab a kicker, grab Ryan Succop. If you've never had him on your team before, you'll see what a treat it is to yell his name. "C'mon Succop!...You got this Succop!....Miss this field goal and I will hunt you down, Succop!" Good times.

2. Any time someone in your league drafts a player on the Titans, just start laughing.

3. Though he only had 63 catches, TE Delanie Walker led the team last year in receptions. Expect that number to rise as Mariota learns the ins and outs of playing QB in the NFL. I'd take him ahead of Dwayne Allen and maybe even Julius Thomas, who could see his numbers decline in Jacksonville this year. Grab him in the 11th round or later.

Is there anything about this team I don't know that I probably should?
Rearrange a few letters of their name and they become the Tennessee Taints.

Enough nonsense, what's your prediction for this season?
Last year's Titans team was one you could run against and score on at will, and it led to a lot of lopsided defeats. Dick LeBeau brings his Steeler pedigree to the defense as an assistant, and the play at linebacker should be better with the return from injury of Zach Brown and free agent signing Brian Orakpo. We'll all be watching to see how Marcus Mariota handles the pro game, but unfortunately for him, he's not surrounded by a lot of talent. Starting wideouts Kendall Wright and Harry Douglass are barely 6'0", and RB tandem Bishop Sankey and (rookie) David Cobb aren't scaring anyone into loading the box. Having the Raiders and Browns on their schedule thanks to last year's fourth place finish helps, but it's still tough to find more than four or five wins unless Mariota is magical right from the start. I expect more of a learning curve, and another high draft pick for Ken Whisenhunt, if they decide to bring him back again in 2016.

The Pro Football Beast Prediction: **3-13**

Your Genius Prediction: _____

DENVER BRONCOS

'14: 12-4 | 1st AFC West | #2 AFC Seed

WK1	BAL	2015 SCHED	
WK 2	@kc	WK 10	KC
WK 3	@det	WK 11	@chi
WK 4	MIN	WK 12	NE
WK 5	@oak	WK 13	@sd
WK 6	@cle	WK 14	OAK
WK 7	BYE	WK 15	@pit
WK 8	GB	WK 16	CIN
WK 9	@ind	WK 17	SD

Claim to Fame: They've allowed only 58 sacks over the last 3 years, fewest in the NFL.

Team Anagram to represent last season:
No Verb Scorned

LOOKING AHEAD TO 2015...

Key Additions: Owen Daniels (BAL), Darian Stewart (BAL), Antonio Smith (OAK), Shane Ray (draft)
Key Subtractions: Julius Thomas (JAX), Terrance Knighton (WAS), Rahim Moore (HOU), Orlando Franklin (SD), Jacob Tamme (ATL)
Key Multiplication: 4 x 31 = 124
Key Division: 39% of the nerves in Payton Manning's neck are frayed or damaged, the other 61% were transplanted from John Elway's neck in a secret procedure this offseason.

(HC) Gary Kubiak, 1st yr | **(DC)** Wade Phillips, 1st yr | **(OC)** Rick Dennison, 1st yr
Base Defense: 3-4

EVERYTHING ELSE YOU NEED TO KNOW...

Do they play in London this year?
Nope. They lost to the 49ers in London in 2010, 24-16.

Do they play in Hamburg this year?
Nope. The NFL does not play games there, but now I'm hungry.

How many prime time games are they scheduled for?
Five, including back to back night games on the road in Weeks 2 and 3.

Do you have any other thoughts on their schedule?
Based on last year's records it's the 11th toughest in the league....a division game in K.C. on three days rest is a tough Week 2 assignment for anyone, especially a new coaching staff...they won't be giving thanks for the schedule in November, when they play the Packers, Colts, and Patriots...after their Week 7 bye, six of their last ten are at home.

EVERYTHING ELSE YOU NEED TO KNOW (CONT'D)...

What is their best-case and worst-case scenario for the season?
Best case, they go 16-0 and win the Super Bowl. Worst case, the entire city gets enveloped in a cloud of cannabis smoke and no one really cares about football anymore and the world runs out of Doritos, which starts World War III, ending life as we know it.

Is there anything about this team I don't know that I probably should?
Terrance Knighton left Denver because he hated the way his butt looked in their pants.

Enough nonsense, what's your prediction for this season?
It's not often that a team coming off a 12-win season shows up with a new coaching staff, but welcome to the 2015 Broncos. The roster remains as solid as anyone in the AFC, but how will they adapt to changes on both sides of the ball? Wade Phillips' new 3-4 scheme will have six games to work out the kinks before a November that brings Rodgers, Luck, and Brady over a critical 5-game stretch. The offense is being asked to learn Gary Kubiak's new scheme without Julius Thomas and LT Ryan Clady, who tore a pec muscle in May. Not sure who Manning will miss more, but the bigger question is whether he'll stay healthy, and I'm not betting on it. Too much change and Advil to repeat as division champs, but as a Wild Card we might get one last Manning-Brady showdown in January.

The Pro Football Beast Prediction: **10-6**

Your Genius Prediction: _____

Predictions from Kickstarter Super Fans...

Matt Gronseth | Doha, Qatar - Peyton leads them to his standard first round bye. The playoffs begin with the horrific neck injury we've all feared. Oz and defense limp them to SB50 where the second hand legal Frisco medicinal herb smoke miraculously heals Peyton's neck AND his chronic case of postseason choking. Champs! PREDICTION: 12-4

Philip Stasyszen | Meeker, OK - I like the Denver Broncos to go 13-3 this year with another year with Peyton Manning. If they can continue with the running game they found at the end of last season, they should win the AFC West without issue.

Austin Gilly | Dallas, TX - Peyton Manning is on a pitch count this year, playing only the 2nd and 4th quarter of every game. Brock "Lobster" Osweiler leads the team in passing yards, but gets hurt in Week 17 when Phillip Rivers accidentally throws one of his kids at him. Tim Tebow is signed and leads the team in rushing yards through the playoffs. Broncos win highest scoring SB ever, Tebow is MVP.

KANSAS CITY CHIEFS

'14: 9-7 | 2nd AFC West | Missed Playoffs

WK1	@hou	2015 SCHED	
WK 2	DEN	WK 10	@den
WK 3	@gb	WK 11	@sd
WK 4	@cin	WK 12	BUF
WK 5	CHI	WK 13	@oak
WK 6	@min	WK 14	SD
WK 7	PIT	WK 15	@bal
WK 8	DET*	WK 16	CLE
WK 9	BYE	WK 17	OAK

Claim to Fame: Their six interceptions in 2014 tied them for fewest in the NFL.

Team Anagram to represent last season:
Eats Icy Fish Snack

LOOKING AHEAD TO 2015...

Key Additions: Jeremy Maclin (PHL), Ben Grubbs (NO), Tyvon Branch (OAK), Marcus Peters (draft)
Key Subtractions: Rodney Hudson (OAK), Vance Walker (DEN), Dwayne Bowe (CLE)
Key Multiplication: 41 x 1 = 41
Key Division: 39% of their passing touchdowns last year were not caught by wide receivers, the other 61% were also not caught by wide receivers.

(HC) Andy Reid, 3rd yr | **(DC)** Bob Sutton, 3rd yr | **(OC)** Doug Pederson, 3rd yr
Base Defense: 3-4

EVERYTHING ELSE YOU NEED TO KNOW...

Do they play in London this year?
Yes. A Week 8 "home game" vs. Detroit at 9:30am ET on Nov. 1.

Do they play on the island from LOST this year?
Nope. Hate to burst your bubble but that is not a real place.

How many prime time games are they scheduled for?
Three, including back to back vs. Denver and at Green Bay in Weeks 2 and 3.

Do you have any other thoughts on their schedule?
Based on last year's records it's the 7th toughest in the league....their only home game in the first four weeks of the season is hosting the Broncos...after their Week 9 bye they have four of five games against division opponents...finishing the season hosting the Browns and Raiders at home is a nice gift from the league in exchange for giving up a home game to London.

EVERYTHING ELSE YOU NEED TO KNOW (CONT'D)...

What is their best-case and worst-case scenario for the season?
Best case, they go 16-0 and win the Super Bowl. Worst case, Andy Reid slathers the entire team in barbecue sauce, cooks them over an open flame, and tries to sell the meat on the black market to Missouri cannibals. The rest of the civilized world revolts against him starting World War III, ending life as we know it.

Can we play a fantasy football version of two lies and a truth?
Sure. One of these points might help you win your fantasy league, two definitely won't.

1. If you want to be the star of your draft, announce that your new team name is "The Kansas City Chefs," then yell, "C'mon in Guy!" and have Guy Fieri waltz into your draft with stacks on stacks of ribs and steaks. The food will be amazing, and Guy Fieri will be so annoying, everyone else will draft a terrible team.

2. Have the 1st pick and want to take Jamaal Charles? Go for it. I'd personally grab Peterson or Lacy before him, but he's in my Top 5 with Le'Veon Bell and Marshawn Lynch.

3. If your league's championship game is Week 16, draft KC's defense with your 2nd overall pick and waste a bench spot on them all year. That Cleveland matchup in Week 16 is juicier than a bruised nectarine.

Is there anything about this team I don't know that I probably should?
HC Andy Reid's bucket list has only 3 things on it: win the Super Bowl, see the Sydney Opera House, and do a shirtless ollie on a skateboard while holding a boombox.

Enough nonsense, what's your prediction for this season?
Now that the Titans have Marcus Mariota, the Chiefs may own the title of 'Most Boring Team in the League'. You've got a QB who doesn't like to throw deep, a coach who doesn't like to take chances, and a defense that was last in the league last year in takeaways. As for bright spots, there are a couple. Travis Kelce, at 6'6" and 260 lbs., has the potential to become the next Gronk if he turns his raw talent into disciplined production. KC's defensive front seven are among the game's best, but a weak secondary has been hurt even more by Sean Smith's three game suspension, making a tough September schedule even tougher. Andy Reid took a 2-14 2012 squad and won 20 games with them in the last two years, but I see regression and a lot more yawning.

The Pro Football Beast Prediction: **7-9**

Your Genius Prediction: _____

SAN DIEGO CHARGERS

'14: 9-7 | 3rd AFC West | Missed Playoffs

		2015 SCHED	
WK1	DET		
WK 2	@cin	WK 10	BYE
WK 3	@min	WK 11	KC
WK 4	CLE	WK 12	@jax
WK 5	PIT	WK 13	DEN
WK 6	@gb	WK 14	@kc
WK 7	OAK	WK 15	MIA
WK 8	@bal	WK 16	@oak
WK 9	CHI	WK 17	@den

Claim to Fame: They had 1,067 defensive penalty yards last season, most in the AFC.

Team Anagram to represent last season: Doing Gas Research

LOOKING AHEAD TO 2015...

Key Additions: Orlando Franklin (DEN), Patrick Robinson (NO), Jacoby Jones (BAL), Melvin Gordon (draft)
Key Subtractions: Ryan Mathews (PHL), Eddie Royal (CHI)
Key Multiplication: 4 x 100 = 400
Key Division: 39% of Philip Rivers' failed 3rd down attempts last year led to him yelling at people as he walked off the field, the other 61% also led to him yelling at people as he walked off the field.

(HC) Mike McCoy, 3rd yr | **(DC)** John Pagano, 4th yr | **(OC)** Frank Reich, 2nd yr
Base Defense: 3-4

EVERYTHING ELSE YOU NEED TO KNOW...

Do they play in London this year?
Nope. They lost to the Saints in London in 2008, 37-32.

Do they play in Addis Ababa this year?
Nope. The NFL does not play games there, you dork.

How many prime time games are they scheduled for?
Four, and the first three of them (Weeks 5, 9, and 11) are at home.

Do you have any other thoughts on their schedule?
Based on last year's records it's the 16th toughest in the league....three of their first six games are against playoff teams from last year...five of their games are currently scheduled for a 10am PT kickoff...five of their last seven games are against divisional opponents...they finish with back to back road games at Oakland and at Denver.

EVERYTHING ELSE YOU NEED TO KNOW (CONT'D)...

What is their best-case and worst-case scenario for the season?
Best case, they go 16-0 and win the Super Bowl. Worst case, the team goes to the beach on an off day and realizes they live in San Diego and why the heck are they playing football anyway when it's so nice out and then Sharknado 4 happens on their beach and they all die.

Can we play a fantasy football version of two lies and a truth?
Sure. One of these points might help you win your fantasy league, two definitely won't.

1. RB Branden Oliver is listed as 208 lbs. in the team's media guide, but my inside sources tells me he's ballooned to 209 lbs. this off-season.

2. Am I the only one bothered by the fact that Nick Novak was born on August 21st? Let's all ban together and pick a different kicker to take a stand against this type of thing.

3. Because of his suspension, TE Antonio Gates has dropped about 45 slots and is being drafted in the 13th round instead of the 9th round. If you're going to wait that long on TE, avoid Gates and try to snag Denver's Owen Daniels in the 11th or 12th round.

Is there anything about this team I don't know that I probably should?
QB Philip Rivers sleeps in velvet footie pajamas with his eyes open and a raccoon puppet on his right hand because he has forty kids. Or eight. One of those is right I think.

Enough nonsense, what's your prediction for this season?
While Winston and Mariota grabbed most of the headlines from the draft this off-season, no team in the league will be impacted more by a rookie than the Chargers. San Diego had a Top-10 passing offense last year, but only two teams were worse on the ground. Melvin Gordon will change all that, taking pressure off Phil Rivers and turning this offense into a threat to score 28 points per game each week. A weak defensive line was not improved in the offseason, but the defense will have to step up if this team wants to win the AFC West. They were fifth worst in the AFC in takeaways last year and dead last in the AFC in penalty yards. With more discipline, and more leads to protect this year, I see them improving enough to get to double-digit wins for the first time since their 13-win season in 2009. Move over Denver, there's a new division champ in town.

The Pro Football Beast Prediction: **10-6**

Your Genius Prediction: _____

OAKLAND RAIDERS

'14: 3-13 | 4th AFC West | Missed Playoffs

WK1	CIN	2015 SCHED	
WK 2	BAL	WK 10	MIN
WK 3	@cle	WK 11	@det
WK 4	@chi	WK 12	@ten
WK 5	DEN	WK 13	KC
WK 6	BYE	WK 14	@den
WK 7	@sd	WK 15	GB
WK 8	NYJ	WK 16	SD
WK 9	@pit	WK 17	@kc

Claim to Fame: They gave up 28.2 PPG, the most in the NFL last year.

Team Anagram to represent last season:
Add Lankier Oars

LOOKING AHEAD TO 2015...

Key Additions: Michael Crabtree (SF), Rodney Hudson (KC), Nate Allen (PHI), Trent Richardson (IND), Amari Cooper (draft)
Key Subtractions: Stefen Wisniewski (JAX), Darren McFadden (DAL), Pat Sims (CIN)
Key Multiplication: 16 x 5 = 80
Key Division: 39% of their season ticket holders have been declared insane, the other 61% were not classified because the doctor ran out of the exam room screaming, "May God help us all!"

(HC) Jack Del Rio, 1st yr | **(DC)** Ken Norton Jr., 1st yr | **(OC)** Bill Musgrave, 1st yr
Base Defense: 4-3

EVERYTHING ELSE YOU NEED TO KNOW...

Do they play in London this year?
Nope. They lost to the Dolphins in London last year, 38-14.

Do they play in the Mines of Moria this year?
Nope. That is a fictional place from the Lord of the Rings.

How many prime time games are they scheduled for?
One, and it is on Christmas Eve hosting the Chargers.

Do you have any other thoughts on their schedule?
Based on last year's records it's the 7th toughest in the league....they start with two games at home, notable because the Raiders are 2-22 on the road since 2012...they will enter December having only payed two division games (Weeks 5 and 7)...all five of their final five games are against teams who finished with a winning record last year.

EVERYTHING ELSE YOU NEED TO KNOW (CONT'D)...

What is their best-case and worst-case scenario for the season?
Best case, they go 1-15. Worst case, they go 0-16.

Can we play a fantasy football version of two lies and a truth?
Sure. One of these points might help you win your fantasy league, two definitely won't.

1. It's his parents' fault, but under no circumstances should you draft Raiders' TE Mychal Rivera based on the spelling of his first name. It's preposterous.

2. I overheard a drunk Raiders fan last week heaping praise on Derek Carr, saying, "...I wouldn't trade him for JJ Watt!" Based on this sage opinion, take him with your first pick.

3. RB Latavius Murray and rookie WR Amari Cooper are both being drafted between rounds 5-7 in standard 10 team leagues. Don't reach before Round 5, but if you can grab either as your RB3/WR3 late in Round 6 or in Round 7, you've done well.

Is there anything about this team I don't know that I probably should?
The black paint used to paint the end zones of the Oakland Coliseum is a proprietary mixture known only by the ghost of Al Davis and MC Hammer. Rumor has it in includes skunk blood, used motor oil, and the tears of orphaned puppies.

Enough nonsense, what's your prediction for this season?
Last year's 3-13 record was a notch below their four-win 2013 campaign, but they are headed in the right direction. Amari Cooper and Michael Crabtree will aid in Derek Carr's development into a serviceable NFL QB, but Carr is still a second year quarterback learning a new offense for the second year in a row. Khalil Mack is a stud, but he's one of eleven guys on a defense that gave up more points than anyone in 2014. They're still below average overall, but they're no longer the dregs of the league.

The Pro Football Beast Prediction: **6-10**

Your Genius Prediction: _____

Predictions from Kickstarter Super Fans...

Chad Gibbs | Auburn, AL - Okay, I'm not sure about the Oakland Raiders, but I can say with some certainty that the Los Angeles Raiders will run roughshod over the rest of the NFL. Why? Two words: Bo Jackson. So long as the Raider's coach (Tom Flores?) always selects Run #2 (Left + A), Bo will score at will and shatter every NFL rushing record by putting up, what some might call, video game numbers.

PART III*
WEEK BY WEEK

*The third part**

(it comes between parts II and IV)*

***I know there's no point in continuing this mediocre footnote gag, but I have to stay committed to this. Besides, anyone who is skipping over these footnotes will miss this important little factoid: in Locker #219 at Case Junior High School in Swansea, Massachusetts there is a key that unlocks a box buried under home plate of the varsity baseball field at the high school containing three dollars, a Gary Sheffield Donruss Rated Rookie Card in Mint Condition, and a few grams of uranium in a plastic baggy. You're welcome.

WEEK 1 (Sep 10th - Sep 14th)

Record results, the betting line, your picks, and home/road/fave/dog trends.
Or if this is too intense for you, just use it for schedule/scores.

WEEK 1 SCHEDULE / RESULTS

ROAD	SCORE	HOME	LINE	MY PICK	W / L	H/R/F/D	TIME (ET)	TV
PIT	-	NE				HF HD RF RD	THU 8:25 PM	NBC
GB	-	CHI				HF HD RF RD	SUN 1:00PM	FOX
KC	-	HOU				HF HD RF RD	SUN 1:00PM	CBS
CLE	-	NYJ				HF HD RF RD	SUN 1:00PM	CBS
IND	-	BUF				HF HD RF RD	SUN 1:00PM	CBS
MIA	-	WAS				HF HD RF RD	SUN 1:00PM	CBS
CAR	-	JAX				HF HD RF RD	SUN 1:00PM	FOX
SEA	-	STL				HF HD RF RD	SUN 1:00PM	FOX
NO	-	ARI				HF HD RF RD	SUN 4:05PM	FOX
DET	-	SD				HF HD RF RD	SUN 4:05PM	FOX
TEN	-	TB				HF HD RF RD	SUN 4:25PM	CBS
CIN	-	OAK				HF HD RF RD	SUN 4:25PM	CBS
BAL	-	DEN				HF HD RF RD	SUN 4:25PM	CBS
NYG	-	DAL				HF HD RF RD	SUN 8:30PM	NBC
PHL	-	ATL				HF HD RF RD	MON 7:10PM	ESPN
MIN	-	SF				HF HD RF RD	MON 10:20PM	ESPN
				TOTALS				

ProFootballBeast Trash Talk Mad Libs

Hey _____, I'm going to rip out your team's heart and smash it to pieces with a _____ this week. I hope a _____ falls on _____ during the pre-game and _____'s arm turns into a _____ in the 1st quarter. Welcome to your worst fantasy season ever. I'd rather eat _____ covered in _____ than have your players. Worst of luck this week, _____

Want to share your own trash talk mad libs?
----------> **GetTheBeastBook.com** <------------

FANTASY TRASH TALK MAD LIBS
Fill in the blanks then post a picture of it on FB, Twitter, or IG. Tag your opponent and use hashtag #PFBTrashTalk.
(We'll highlight best ones each week.)

Help for the 9 blanks to fill in:
1: Fantasy Owner you're facing this wk
2: a tool or weapon
3: a heavy object
4: an opposing fantasy WR
5: the opposing fantasy QB
6: a random object
7: something nasty
8: another something nasty
9: You (or your fantasy team name

WEEKLY GAME

Complete, then snap a picture & share on FB, IG, or Twitter. Hashtag: #PFBPropGame

Entry must be posted: Between Thursday 9/10 & Sunday 9/13 by 9am. (Eastern Time)

All 10 right, win prize listed on website.

7 or more right, earn one grand prize entry per rules on website.

Details, official rules at ProFootballBeast.com

ProFootballBeast Prop Game For Week 1

1) Who wins, TEN or TB?	TEN	TB
2) Total Passing Yards for IND?	<301.5	>301.5
3) Total points in SEA/STL game?	<43.5	>43.5
4) Name the Top Fantasy QB on Sun/Mon?	_____	
5) Who wins, DET or SD?	DET	SD
6) Total ostriches on CIN sideline?	0	>0
7) Total # INTs in NYG/DAL game?	<2.5	>2.5
8) Highest Scoring Team on Sun/Mon?	_____	
9) Total Yards for PHL?	<351.5	>351.5
10) Who wins, MIN or SF?	MIN	SF

EXTRAS:
Bold prediction of the week: _____
How many fantasy leagues are you in: _____
Who drafted the worst team in your league: _____

Link to winning entries must emailed to PFB for it to count. Full submission details at ProFootballBeast.com/weeklygame/ Want to play? Get yourself a copy ----> **GetTheBeastBook.com**

YOUR POWER POLL

Fill in your rankings, snap a picture, and share on social this week. Use the hashtag: #PFBPowerPoll

WEEK 1 NOTES:

_____
_____
_____
_____
_____
_____
_____

MY NFL POWER POLL FOR WEEK 1

TOP 5 TEAMS   BOTTOM 5 TEAMS
1._____   32._____
2._____   31._____
3._____   30._____
4._____   29._____
5._____   28._____

YOUR TOP 3 SB50 MATCH-UP PREDICTIONS
   1._____
   2._____
   3._____

To share your own power poll, get the book!
-----------------> **GetTheBeastBook.com** <--------------------

WEEK 2 (Sep 17th - Sep 21st)

Record results, the betting line, your picks, and home/road/fave/dog trends.
Or if this is too intense for you, just use it for schedule/scores.

WEEK 2 SCHEDULE / RESULTS

ROAD	SCORE	HOME	LINE	MY PICK	W / L	H/R/F/D	TIME (ET)	TV
DEN	-	KC				HF HD RF RD	THU 8:25 PM	CBS
HOU	-	CAR				HF HD RF RD	SUN 1:00PM	CBS
SF	-	PIT				HF HD RF RD	SUN 1:00PM	FOX
TB	-	NO				HF HD RF RD	SUN 1:00PM	FOX
DET	-	MIN				HF HD RF RD	SUN 1:00PM	FOX
ARI	-	CHI				HF HD RF RD	SUN 1:00PM	FOX
NE	-	BUF				HF HD RF RD	SUN 1:00PM	CBS
SD	-	CIN				HF HD RF RD	SUN 1:00PM	CBS
TEN	-	CLE				HF HD RF RD	SUN 1:00PM	CBS
ATL	-	NYG				HF HD RF RD	SUN 1:00PM	FOX
STL	-	WAS				HF HD RF RD	SUN 1:00PM	FOX
MIA	-	JAX				HF HD RF RD	SUN 4:05PM	CBS
BAL	-	OAK				HF HD RF RD	SUN 4:05PM	CBS
DAL	-	PHL				HF HD RF RD	SUN 4:25PM	FOX
SEA	-	GB				HF HD RF RD	SUN 8:30PM	NBC
NYJ	-	IND				HF HD RF RD	MON 8:30PM	ESPN
				TOTALS				

ProFootballBeast Trash Talk Mad Libs

Hey _____, nice team you got there! I'd rather start _____ or a _____ on my team than start _____. Too bad our league doesn't give points for looking like a mangled _____, because your face would be undefeated. I hope _____'s _____ explodes during the national anthem. Get ready to lose by _____ points. Sincerely, _____.

Want to share your own trash talk mad libs?
----------> GetTheBeastBook.com <------------

FANTASY TRASH TALK MAD LIBS

Fill in the blanks then post a picture of it on FB, Twitter, or IG. Tag your opponent and use hashtag #PFBTrashTalk.
(We'll highlight best ones each week.)

Help for the 9 blanks to fill in:
1: Fantasy Owner you're facing this wk
2: any cartoon character
3: any inanimate object
4: worst guy on your opponent's team
5: an animal your opponent looks like
6: a stud on your opponent's team
7: a body part
8: a number between 150-250
9: You (or your fantasy team name)

WEEKLY GAME

Complete, then snap a picture & share on FB, IG, or Twitter. Hashtag: #PFBPropGame

Entry must be posted: Between Thursday 9/17 & Sunday 9/20 by 9am. (Eastern Time)

All 10 right, win prize listed on website.

7 or more right, earn one grand prize entry per rules on website.

Details, official rules at ProFootballBeast.com

ProFootballBeast Prop Game For Week 2

1) Who wins, SD or CIN?	SD	CIN
2) Total Passing Yards for BAL?	<261.5	>261.5
3) Total points in TEN/CLE game?	<37.5	>37.5
4) Name 1 of Top 2 fantasy RBs on Sun/Mon?	_____	
5) Who wins, DAL or PHL?	DAL	PHL
6) Largest lead in BAL/OAK game?	<14.5	>14.5
7) Total referee fistfights during NE/BUF?	0	>0
8) Highest Scoring Team on Sun/Mon?	_____	
9) Longest TD (yds) in SF/PIT game?	<39.5	>39.5
10) Who wins, SEA or GB?	SEA	GB

EXTRAS:

Bold prediction of the week: _____

Worst person to watch NFL w/ this wk: _____

Current NFL player you can probably beat up: _____

Link to winning entries must emailed to PFB for it to count. Full submission details at ProFootballBeast.com/weeklygame/
Want to play? Get yourself a copy ---> **GetTheBeastBook.com**

YOUR POWER POLL

Fill in your rankings, snap a picture, and share on social this week. Use the hashtag: #PFBPowerPoll

WEEK 2 NOTES:

_____
_____
_____
_____
_____
_____
_____

MY NFL POWER POLL FOR WEEK 2

TOP 5 TEAMS   BOTTOM 5 TEAMS

1. _____   32. _____
2. _____   31. _____
3. _____   30. _____
4. _____   29. _____
5. _____   28. _____

YOUR 3 LEAST FAVORITE NFL ANNOUNCERS

1. _____
2. _____
3. _____

To share your own power poll, get the book!
----------> **GetTheBeastBook.com** <----------

WEEK 3 (Sep 24th - Sep 28th)

Record results, the betting line, your picks, and home/road/fave/dog trends.
Or if this is too intense for you, just use it for schedule/scores.

WEEK 3 SCHEDULE / RESULTS

ROAD	SCORE	HOME	LINE	MY PICK	W/L	H/R/F/D	TIME (ET)	TV
WAS	-	NYG				HF HD RF RD	THU 8:25 PM	CBS
ATL	-	DAL				HF HD RF RD	SUN 1:00PM	FOX
IND	-	TEN				HF HD RF RD	SUN 1:00PM	CBS
OAK	-	CLE				HF HD RF RD	SUN 1:00PM	CBS
CIN	-	BAL				HF HD RF RD	SUN 1:00PM	CBS
JAX	-	NE				HF HD RF RD	SUN 1:00PM	CBS
NO	-	CAR				HF HD RF RD	SUN 1:00PM	FOX
PHL	-	NYJ				HF HD RF RD	SUN 1:00PM	FOX
TB	-	HOU				HF HD RF RD	SUN 1:00PM	FOX
SD	-	MIN				HF HD RF RD	SUN 1:00PM	CBS
PIT	-	STL				HF HD RF RD	SUN 1:00PM	CBS
SF	-	ARI				HF HD RF RD	SUN 4:05PM	FOX
BUF	-	MIA				HF HD RF RD	SUN 4:25PM	CBS
CHI	-	SEA				HF HD RF RD	SUN 4:25PM	CBS
DEN	-	DET				HF HD RF RD	SUN 8:30PM	NBC
KC	-	GB				HF HD RF RD	MON 8:30PM	ESPN
				TOTALS				

ProFootballBeast Trash Talk Mad Libs

Hey _____, I'm going to rip out your team's _____ and smash it to pieces with a _____ this week. _____ is going to make you beg for mercy. Your team smells like _____ mixed with _____ feces. I'd rather never play fantasy again than have your roster. Why _____, was _____ not available? May you never win a game again in this or any season, _____.

Want to share your own trash talk mad libs?
----------> **GetTheBeastBook.com** <------------

FANTASY TRASH TALK MAD LIBS
Fill in the blanks then post a picture of it on FB, Twitter, or IG. Tag your opponent and use hashtag #PFBTrashTalk.
(We'll highlight best ones each week.)

Help for the 9 blanks to fill in:
1: Fantasy Owner you're facing this wk
2: internal organ
3: any object
4: one of your best players
5: something gross
6: an animal
7: your opponent's worst player
8: retired player from the 80s or 90s
9: You (or your fantasy team name)

WEEKLY GAME

Complete, then snap a picture & share on FB, IG, or Twitter. Hashtag: #PFBPropGame

Entry must be posted: Between Thursday 9/24 & Sunday 9/27 by 9am. (Eastern Time)

All 10 right, win prize listed on website.

7 or more right, earn one grand prize entry per rules on website.

Details, official rules at ProFootballBeast.com

ProFootballBeast Prop Game For Week 3

1) Who wins, NO or CAR?	NO	CAR
2) Total Rushing Yards for NE?	<109.5	>109.5
3) Total home runs in NE/BUF game?	0	>0
4) Top Fantasy QB on Sun/Mon?		
5) Who wins, BUF or MIA?	BUF	MIA
6) Longest FG in PIT/STL game?	<34.5	>34.5
7) Total # INTs in OAK/CLE game?	<3.5	>3.5
8) Highest Scoring Team on Sun/Mon?		
9) Points scored in 1st Q of KC/GB?	<14.5	>14.5
10) Who wins, DEN or DET?	DEN	DET

EXTRAS:
Bold prediction of the week: _____
Worst fantasy player in your league: _____
Most overrated NFL football player: _____

Link to winning entries must emailed to PFB for it to count. Full submission details at ProFootballBeast.com/weeklygame/
Want to play? Get yourself a copy ---> **GetTheBeastBook.com**

YOUR POWER POLL

Fill in your rankings, snap a picture, and share on social this week. Use the hashtag: #PFBPowerPoll

WEEK 3 NOTES:
_____
_____
_____
_____
_____
_____
_____

MY NFL POWER POLL FOR WEEK 3

TOP 5 TEAMS	BOTTOM 5 TEAMS
1._____	32._____
2._____	31._____
3._____	30._____
4._____	29._____
5._____	28._____

YOUR TOP 3 GAME TIME FOOTBALL SNACKS
1._____
2._____
3._____

To share your own power poll, get the book!
--------------> **GetTheBeastBook.com** <--------------

WEEK 4 (Oct 1st - Oct 5th)

Record results, the betting line, your picks, and home/road/fave/dog trends.
Or if this is too intense for you, just use it for schedule/scores.

WEEK 4 SCHEDULE / RESULTS

BYE: TEN, NE | ***LONDON:** NYJ @ MIA - SUN, 9:30AM ET

ROAD	SCORE	HOME	LINE	MY PICK	W/L	H/R/F/D	TIME (ET)	TV
BAL	-	PIT				HF HD RF RD	THU 8:25 PM	CBS
NYJ	-	MIA*				HF HD RF RD	SUN 9:30AM	CBS
JAX	-	IND				HF HD RF RD	SUN 1:00PM	CBS
NYG	-	BUF				HF HD RF RD	SUN 1:00PM	FOX
CAR	-	TB				HF HD RF RD	SUN 1:00PM	FOX
PHL	-	WAS				HF HD RF RD	SUN 1:00PM	FOX
OAK	-	CHI				HF HD RF RD	SUN 1:00PM	CBS
HOU	-	ATL				HF HD RF RD	SUN 1:00PM	CBS
KC	-	CIN				HF HD RF RD	SUN 1:00PM	CBS
CLE	-	SD				HF HD RF RD	SUN 4:05PM	CBS
GB	-	SF				HF HD RF RD	SUN 4:25PM	FOX
STL	-	ARI				HF HD RF RD	SUN 4:25PM	FOX
MIN	-	DEN				HF HD RF RD	SUN 4:25PM	FOX
DAL	-	NO				HF HD RF RD	SUN 8:30PM	NBC
DET	-	SEA				HF HD RF RD	MON 8:30PM	ESPN
				TOTALS				

ProFootballBeast Trash Talk Mad Libs

Hey _____, get ready to hate _____ because he's going to smash you in the _____ with a bag of _____ all day. Why is _____ on your roster? You know we don't get points for injuries, right? I hope _____ gets trampled by a runaway _____ during the coin toss. Remember when you drafted _____? That's when I knew you sucked. Worst of luck, _____.

Want to share your own trash talk mad libs?
----------> **GetTheBeastBook.com** <-----------

FANTASY TRASH TALK MAD LIBS
Fill in the blanks then post a picture of it on FB, Twitter, or IG. Tag your opponent and use hashtag #PFBTrashTalk.
(We'll highlight best ones each week.)

Help for the 9 blanks to fill in:
1: Fantasy Owner you're facing this wk
2: your best player this week
3: body part
4: random object (plural)
5: injured guy on roster (or injury prone)
6: your opponent's best player
7: large animal
8: opponent's worst pick (research it)
9: You (or your fantasy team name)

WEEKLY GAME

Complete, then snap a picture & share on FB, IG, or Twitter. Hashtag: #PFBPropGame

Entry must be posted: Between Thursday 10/1 & Sunday 10/4 by 9am. (Eastern Time)

All 10 right, win prize listed on website.

7 or more right, earn one grand prize entry per rules on website.

Details, official rules at ProFootballBeast.com

ProFootballBeast Prop Game For Week 4

1) Who wins, NYG or BUF?	NYG	BUF
2) Longest TD in PHL/WAS game?	<39.5	>39.5
3) Total points in JAX/IND game?	<44.5	>44.5
4) Name 1 of Top 3 fantasy WRs on Sun/Mon?	_____	
5) Who wins, GB or SF?	GB	SF
6) Total bear maulings during KC/CIN?	0	>0
7) Total Punt return TDs on Sunday?	<1.5	>1.5
8) Highest Scoring Team on Sun/Mon?	_____	
9) Total made FGs in DAL/NO game?	<3.5	>3.5
10) Who wins, DET or SEA?	DET	SEA

EXTRAS:
Bold prediction of the week: _____
Most football-obsessed person you know: _____
Pro football team you hate the most: _____

Link to winning entries must emailed to PFB for it to count.
Full submission details at ProFootballBeast.com/weeklygame/
Want to play? Get yourself a copy ---> **GetTheBeastBook.com**

YOUR POWER POLL

Fill in your rankings, snap a picture, and share on social this week. Use the hashtag: #PFBPowerPoll

WEEK 4 NOTES:

_____
_____
_____
_____
_____
_____
_____

MY NFL POWER POLL FOR WEEK 4

TOP 5 TEAMS   BOTTOM 5 TEAMS
1._____   32._____
2._____   31._____
3._____   30._____
4._____   29._____
5._____   28._____

YOUR TOP 3 WIDE RECEIVER RANKINGS
   1._____
   2._____
   3._____

To share your own power poll, get the book!
-----------------> **GetTheBeastBook.com** <-----------------

WEEK 5 (Oct 8th - Oct 12th)

Record results, the betting line, your picks, and home/road/fave/dog trends.
Or if this is too intense for you, just use it for schedule/scores.

WEEK 5 SCHEDULE / RESULTS

BYE: MIA, MIN, NYJ, CAR

ROAD	SCORE	HOME	LINE	MY PICK	W/L	H/R/F/D	TIME (ET)	TV
IND	-	HOU				HF HD RF RD	THU 8:25 PM	CBS
CHI	-	KC				HF HD RF RD	SUN 1:00PM	FOX
SEA	-	CIN				HF HD RF RD	SUN 1:00PM	FOX
WAS	-	ATL				HF HD RF RD	SUN 1:00PM	FOX
JAX	-	TB				HF HD RF RD	SUN 1:00PM	CBS
NO	-	PHL				HF HD RF RD	SUN 1:00PM	FOX
CLE	-	BAL				HF HD RF RD	SUN 1:00PM	CBS
STL	-	GB				HF HD RF RD	SUN 1:00PM	CBS
BUF	-	TEN				HF HD RF RD	SUN 1:00PM	CBS
ARI	-	DET				HF HD RF RD	SUN 4:05PM	FOX
NE	-	DAL				HF HD RF RD	SUN 4:25PM	CBS
DEN	-	OAK				HF HD RF RD	SUN 4:25PM	CBS
SF	-	NYG				HF HD RF RD	SUN 8:30PM	NBC
PIT	-	SD				HF HD RF RD	MON 8:30PM	ESPN
SUN GAMES MAY BE FLEXED TO 8:30				TOTALS				

ProFootballBeast Trash Talk Mad Libs

Hey _____, I'm going to rip out your team's soul and break it to pieces with a _____ this week. I hope a _____ falls on _____ during the pre-game and _____'s arm turns into a _____ in the 1st quarter. Prepare to go on a very long losing streak. I'd rather eat _____ covered in _____ than have your players. Worst of luck this week, _____

Want to share your own trash talk mad libs?
----------> GetTheBeastBook.com <------------

FANTASY TRASH TALK MAD LIBS
Fill in the blanks then post a picture of it on FB, Twitter, or IG. Tag your opponent and use hashtag #PFBTrashTalk.
(We'll highlight best ones each week.)

Help for the 9 blanks to fill in:
1: Fantasy Owner you're facing this wk
2: a tool or weapon
3: a heavy object
4: an opposing fantasy WR
5: the opposing fantasy QB
6: a random object
7: something nasty
8: another something nasty
9: You (or your fantasy team name

WEEKLY GAME

Complete, then snap a picture & share on FB, IG, or Twitter. Hashtag: #PFBPropGame

Entry must be posted: Between Thursday 10/8 & Sunday 10/11 by 9am (Eastern Time)

All 10 right, win prize listed on website.

7 or more right, earn one grand prize entry per rules on website.

Details, official rules at ProFootballBeast.com

ProFootballBeast Prop Game For Week 5

1) Who wins, CHI or KC?	CHI	KC
2) Total Passing Yards for CIN?	<231.5	>231.5
3) Total blades of grass on GB's field?	<5.5	>5.5
4) Top Fantasy QB on Sun/Mon?		
5) Who wins, NE or DAL?	NE	DAL
6) Total Rushing Yards for BUF?	<111.5	>111.5
7) Total # INTs in JAX/TB game?	<3.5	>3.5
8) Highest Scoring Team on Sun/Mon?		
9) Total Yards for NYG?	<381.5	>381.5
10) Who wins, PIT or SD?	PIT	SD

EXTRAS:
Bold prediction of the week: _____
Are you undefeated in any of your fantasy leagues: _____
Player you regret drafting the most for fantasy: _____

Link to winning entries must emailed to PFB for it to count. Full submission details at ProFootballBeast.com/weeklygame/
Want to play? Get yourself a copy ---> **GetTheBeastBook.com**

YOUR POWER POLL

Fill in your rankings, snap a picture, and share on social this week. Use the hashtag: #PFBPowerPoll

WEEK 5 NOTES:

_____
_____
_____
_____
_____
_____
_____

MY NFL POWER POLL FOR WEEK 5

TOP 5 TEAMS   BOTTOM 5 TEAMS
1._____   32._____
2._____   31._____
3._____   30._____
4._____   29._____
5._____   28._____

YOUR TOP 3 MVP CANDIDATES RIGHT NOW
   1._____
   2._____
   3._____

To share your own power poll, get the book!
-----------> **GetTheBeastBook.com** <-----------

WEEK 6 (Oct 15th - Oct 19th)

Record results, the betting line, your picks, and home/road/fave/dog trends.
Or if this is too intense for you, just use it for schedule/scores.

WEEK 6 SCHEDULE / RESULTS

BYE: DAL, OAK, STL, TB

ROAD	SCORE	HOME	LINE	MY PICK	W/L	H/R/F/D	TIME (ET)	TV
ATL	-	NO				HF HD RF RD	THU 8:25 PM	CBS
WAS	-	NYJ				HF HD RF RD	SUN 1:00PM	FOX
ARI	-	PIT				HF HD RF RD	SUN 1:00PM	FOX
KC	-	MIN				HF HD RF RD	SUN 1:00PM	CBS
CIN	-	BUF				HF HD RF RD	SUN 1:00PM	CBS
CHI	-	DET				HF HD RF RD	SUN 1:00PM	FOX
DEN	-	CLE				HF HD RF RD	SUN 1:00PM	CBS
HOU	-	JAX				HF HD RF RD	SUN 1:00PM	CBS
MIA	-	TEN				HF HD RF RD	SUN 1:00PM	CBS
CAR	-	SEA				HF HD RF RD	SUN 4:05PM	FOX
SD	-	GB				HF HD RF RD	SUN 4:25PM	CBS
BAL	-	SF				HF HD RF RD	SUN 4:25PM	CBS
NE	-	IND				HF HD RF RD	SUN 8:30PM	NBC
NYG	-	PHL				HF HD RF RD	MON 8:30PM	ESPN
SUN GAMES MAY BE FLEXED TO 8:30				TOTALS				

ProFootballBeast Trash Talk Mad Libs

Hey _____, nice team you got there! I'd rather start _____ or a _____ on my team than start _____. Too bad our league doesn't give points for looking like a mangled _____, because your face would be undefeated. I hope _____'s _____ explodes during the pre-game. Get ready to lose by _____ points. Sincerely, _____

Want to share your own trash talk mad libs?
----------> GetTheBeastBook.com <-----------

FANTASY TRASH TALK MAD LIBS

Fill in the blanks then post a picture of it on FB, Twitter, or IG. Tag your opponent and use hashtag #PFBTrashTalk.
(We'll highlight best ones each week.)

Help for the 9 blanks to fill in:
1: Fantasy Owner you're facing this wk
2: a retired/old football player
3: any inanimate object
4: worst guy on your opponent's team
5: an animal your opponent looks like
6: a stud on your opponent's team
7: a body part
8: a number between 150-250
9: You (or your fantasy team name)

WEEKLY GAME

Complete, then snap a picture & share on FB, IG, or Twitter. Hashtag: #PFBPropGame

Entry must be posted: Between Thurs. 10/15 & Sun. 10/18 by 9am. (Eastern Time)

All 10 right, win prize listed on website.

7 or more right, earn one grand prize entry per rules on website.

Details, official rules at ProFootballBeast.com

ProFootballBeast Prop Game For Week 6

1) Who wins, CHI or DET?	CHI	DET
2) Largest lead in KC/MIN game?	<13.5	>13.5
3) Total points in WAS/NYJ game?	<39.5	>39.5
4) Name 1 of Top 2 fantasy RBs on Sun/Mon?	_____	
5) Who wins, BAL or SF?	BAL	SF
6) Total Rushing Yards for SEA?	<145.5	>145.5
7) Total piggyback ride TDs in ARI/PIT game?	0	>0
8) Highest Scoring Team on Sun/Mon?	_____	
9) Longest TD (yds) in SD/GB game?	<39.5	>39.5
10) Who wins, NYG or PHL?	NYG	PHL

EXTRAS:
Bold prediction of the week: _____
What PSI will Tom Brady's balls be at this week: _____
Head coach that will get fired first: _____

Link to winning entries must emailed to PFB for it to count.
Full submission details at ProFootballBeast.com/weeklygame/
Want to play? Get yourself a copy ---> **GetTheBeastBook.com**

YOUR POWER POLL

Fill in your rankings, snap a picture, and share on social this week. Use the hashtag: #PFBPowerPoll

WEEK 6 NOTES:

_____
_____
_____
_____
_____
_____
_____

MY NFL POWER POLL FOR WEEK 6

TOP 5 TEAMS   BOTTOM 5 TEAMS
1._____   32._____
2._____   31._____
3._____   30._____
4._____   29._____
5._____   28._____

YOUR TOP 3 SHOWS ON TV RIGHT NOW
  1._____
  2._____
  3._____

To share your own power poll, get the book!
--------------> **GetTheBeastBook.com** <--------------

WEEK 7 (Oct 22nd - Oct 26th)

Record results, the betting line, your picks, and home/road/fave/dog trends.
Or if this is too intense for you, just use it for schedule/scores.

WEEK 7 SCHEDULE / RESULTS

BYE: CHI, CIN, DEN, GB | *LONDON: BUF @ JAX - SUN, 9:30AM ET (DIGITAL ONLY - YAHOO!)

ROAD	SCORE	HOME	LINE	MY PICK	W / L	H/R/F/D	TIME (ET)	TV
SEA	-	SF				HF HD RF RD	THU 8:25 PM	CBS
BUF	-	JAX*				HF HD RF RD	SUN 9:30AM	YAHOO!
TB	-	WAS				HF HD RF RD	SUN 1:00PM	FOX
ATL	-	TEN				HF HD RF RD	SUN 1:00PM	FOX
NO	-	IND				HF HD RF RD	SUN 1:00PM	FOX
MIN	-	DET				HF HD RF RD	SUN 1:00PM	FOX
PIT	-	KC				HF HD RF RD	SUN 1:00PM	CBS
CLE	-	STL				HF HD RF RD	SUN 1:00PM	CBS
HOU	-	MIA				HF HD RF RD	SUN 1:00PM	CBS
NYJ	-	NE				HF HD RF RD	SUN 1:00PM	CBS
OAK	-	SD				HF HD RF RD	SUN 4:05PM	CBS
DAL	-	NYG				HF HD RF RD	SUN 4:25PM	FOX
PHL	-	CAR				HF HD RF RD	SUN 8:30PM	NBC
BAL	-	ARI				HF HD RF RD	MON 8:30PM	ESPN
SUN GAMES MAY BE FLEXED TO 8:30				TOTALS				

ProFootballBeast Trash Talk Mad Libs

Hey _____, I'm going to rip out your team's _____ and smash it to pieces with a _____ this week. _____ is going to make you beg for mercy. Your team smells like _____ mixed with _____ turds. I'd rather never play fantasy again than have your roster. Why _____, was _____ not available? May you never win a game again in this or any season, _____.

Want to share your own trash talk mad libs?
----------> GetTheBeastBook.com <------------

FANTASY TRASH TALK MAD LIBS
Fill in the blanks then post a picture of it on FB, Twitter, or IG. Tag your opponent and use hashtag #PFBTrashTalk.
(We'll highlight best ones each week.)

Help for the 9 blanks to fill in:
1: Fantasy Owner you're facing this wk
2: internal organ
3: any object
4: one of your best players
5: something gross
6: an animal
7: your opponent's worst player
8: retired player from the 80s or 90s
9: You (or your fantasy team name)

WEEKLY GAME

Complete, then snap a picture & share on FB, IG, or Twitter. Hashtag: #PFBPropGame

Entry must be posted: Between Thurs. 10/22 & Sun. 10/25 by 9am. (Eastern Time)

All 10 right, win prize listed on website.

7 or more right, earn one grand prize entry per rules on website.

Details, official rules at ProFootballBeast.com

ProFootballBeast Prop Game For Week 7

1) Who wins, ATL or TEN?	ATL	TEN
2) Total alien abductions during SEA/SF?	0	>0
3) Total points in PIT/KC game?	<49.5	>49.5
4) Top Fantasy QB on Sun/Mon?	_____	
5) Who wins, DAL or NYG?	DAL	NYG
6) Longest FG in CLE/STL game?	<35.5	>35.5
7) Total # INTs in ATL/TEN game?	<3.5	>3.5
8) Highest Scoring Team on Sun/Mon?	_____	
9) Points scored in 4th Q of OAK/SD?	<13.5	>13.5
10) Who wins, BAL or ARI?	BAL	ARI

EXTRAS:
Bold prediction of the week: _____
Worst fantasy owner in your league so far: _____
Worst coach in the NFL so far this year: _____

Link to winning entries must emailed to PFB for it to count. Full submission details at ProFootballBeast.com/weeklygame/
Want to play? Get yourself a copy ---> **GetTheBeastBook.com**

YOUR POWER POLL

Fill in your rankings, snap a picture, and share on social this week. Use the hashtag: #PFBPowerPoll

WEEK 7 NOTES:

_____
_____
_____
_____
_____
_____

MY NFL POWER POLL FOR WEEK 7

TOP 5 TEAMS   BOTTOM 5 TEAMS
1._____   32._____
2._____   31._____
3._____   30._____
4._____   29._____
5._____   28._____

YOUR TOP 3 GUESSES FOR FIRST HEAD COACH FIRED
   1._____
   2._____
   3._____

To share your own power poll, get the book!
-----------------> **GetTheBeastBook.com** <--------------------

WEEK 8 (Oct 29th - Nov 2nd)

Record results, the betting line, your picks, and home/road/fave/dog trends.
Or if this is too intense for you, just use it for schedule/scores.

WEEK 8 SCHEDULE / RESULTS

BYE: BUF, PHL, WAS, JAX | ***LONDON:** DET @ KC - SUN, 9:30AM ET

ROAD	SCORE	HOME	LINE	MY PICK	W/L	H/R/F/D	TIME (ET)	TV
MIA	-	NE				HF HD RF RD	THU 8:25 PM	CBS
DET	-	KC				HF HD RF RD	SUN 9:30AM	FOX
TB	-	ATL				HF HD RF RD	SUN 1:00PM	FOX
ARI	-	CLE				HF HD RF RD	SUN 1:00PM	FOX
SF	-	STL				HF HD RF RD	SUN 1:00PM	FOX
NYG	-	NO				HF HD RF RD	SUN 1:00PM	FOX
MIN	-	CHI				HF HD RF RD	SUN 1:00PM	FOX
SD	-	BAL				HF HD RF RD	SUN 1:00PM	CBS
CIN	-	PIT				HF HD RF RD	SUN 1:00PM	CBS
TEN	-	HOU				HF HD RF RD	SUN 1:00PM	CBS
NYJ	-	OAK				HF HD RF RD	SUN 4:05PM	CBS
SEA	-	DAL				HF HD RF RD	SUN 4:25PM	FOX
GB	-	DEN				HF HD RF RD	SUN 8:30PM	NBC
IND	-	CAR				HF HD RF RD	MON 8:30PM	ESPN
SUN GAMES MAY BE FLEXED TO 8:30				TOTALS				

ProFootballBeast Trash Talk Mad Libs

Hey _____, get ready to hate _____ because he's going to smash you in the _____ with a bag of _____ all day. Why is _____ on your roster? You know we don't get points for injuries, right? I hope _____ gets eaten by a rabid _____ during the coin toss. Remember when you drafted _____? That's when I knew you sucked. Worst of luck, _____.

Want to share your own trash talk mad libs?
----------> **GetTheBeastBook.com** <-----------

FANTASY TRASH TALK MAD LIBS
Fill in the blanks then post a picture of it on FB, Twitter, or IG. Tag your opponent and use hashtag #PFBTrashTalk.
(We'll highlight best ones each week.)

Help for the 9 blanks to fill in:
1: Fantasy Owner you're facing this wk
2: your best player this week
3: body part
4: random object (plural)
5: injured guy on roster (or injury prone)
6: your opponent's best player
7: wild animal
8: opponent's worst pick (research it)
9: You (or your fantasy team name)

WEEKLY GAME

Complete, then snap a picture & share on FB, IG, or Twitter. Hashtag: #PFBPropGame

Entry must be posted: Between Thurs. 10/29 & Sun. 11/1 by 9am. (Eastern Time)

All 10 right, win prize listed on website.

7 or more right, earn one grand prize entry per rules on website.

Details, official rules at ProFootballBeast.com

ProFootballBeast Prop Game For Week 8

1) Who wins, NYG or NO?	NYG	NO
2) Longest TD in ARI/CLE game?	<39.5	>39.5
3) Total points in SF/STL game?	<42.5	>42.5
4) Name 1 of Top 3 fantasy WRs on Sun/Mon?	_____	
5) Who wins, SD or BAL?	SD	BAL
6) Total Yards for DAL?	<369.5	>369.5
7) Total # fans wearing face paint in OAK?	<1.5	>1.5
8) Highest Scoring Team on Sun/Mon?	_____	
9) Total made FGs in GB/DEN game?	<3.5	>3.5
10) Who wins, IND or CAR?	IND	CAR

EXTRAS:
Bold prediction of the week: _____
Most football-obsessed person you know: _____
Pro football team you hate the most: _____

*Link to winning entries must emailed to PFB for it to count. Full submission details at ProFootballBeast.com/weeklygame/ Want to play? Get yourself a copy ---> **GetTheBeastBook.com***

YOUR POWER POLL

Fill in your rankings, snap a picture, and share on social this week. Use the hashtag: #PFBPowerPoll

WEEK 8 NOTES:

_____
_____
_____
_____
_____
_____
_____

MY NFL POWER POLL FOR WEEK 8

TOP 5 TEAMS   BOTTOM 5 TEAMS
1._____   32._____
2._____   31._____
3._____   30._____
4._____   29._____
5._____   28._____

YOUR TOP 3 HALLOWEEN COSTUME IDEAS
  1._____
  2._____
  3._____

To share your own power poll, get the book!
--------------> **GetTheBeastBook.com** <--------------

WEEK 9 (Nov 5th - Nov 9th)

Record results, the betting line, your picks, and home/road/fave/dog trends.
Or if this is too intense for you, just use it for schedule/scores.

WEEK 9 SCHEDULE / RESULTS

BYE: DET, KC, ARI, SEA, BAL, HOU

ROAD	SCORE	HOME	LINE	MY PICK	W/L	H/R/F/D	TIME (ET)	TV
CLE	-	CIN				HF HD RF RD	THU 8:25 PM	NFL
GB	-	CAR				HF HD RF RD	SUN 1:00PM	FOX
WAS	-	NE				HF HD RF RD	SUN 1:00PM	FOX
TEN	-	NO				HF HD RF RD	SUN 1:00PM	CBS
MIA	-	BUF				HF HD RF RD	SUN 1:00PM	CBS
STL	-	MIN				HF HD RF RD	SUN 1:00PM	FOX
JAX	-	NYJ				HF HD RF RD	SUN 1:00PM	CBS
OAK	-	PIT				HF HD RF RD	SUN 1:00PM	CBS
NYG	-	TB				HF HD RF RD	SUN 4:05PM	FOX
ATL	-	SF				HF HD RF RD	SUN 4:05PM	FOX
DEN	-	IND				HF HD RF RD	SUN 4:25PM	CBS
PHL	-	DAL				HF HD RF RD	SUN 8:30PM	NBC
CHI	-	SD				HF HD RF RD	MON 8:30PM	ESPN
SUN GAMES MAY BE FLEXED TO 8:30				TOTALS				

ProFootballBeast Trash Talk Mad Libs

Hey _____, I'm going to rip out your team's spirit and smash it to pieces with a _____ this week. I hope a _____ falls on _____ during the pre-game and _____'s arm turns into a _____ in the 1st quarter. Any wins you have are 100% from luck. I'd rather eat _____ covered in _____ than have your players. Worst of luck this week, _____.

Want to share your own trash talk mad libs?
----------> **GetTheBeastBook.com** <------------

FANTASY TRASH TALK MAD LIBS
Fill in the blanks then post a picture of it on FB, Twitter, or IG. Tag your opponent and use hashtag #PFBTrashTalk.
(We'll highlight best ones each week.)

Help for the 9 blanks to fill in:
1: Fantasy Owner you're facing this wk
2: a tool or weapon
3: a heavy object
4: an opposing fantasy WR
5: the opposing fantasy QB
6: a random object
7: something nasty
8: another something nasty
9: You (or your fantasy team name

WEEKLY GAME

Complete, then snap a picture & share on FB, IG, or Twitter. Hashtag: #PFBPropGame

Entry must be posted: Between Thurs. 11/5 & Sun. 11/8 by 9am. (Eastern Time)

All 10 right, win prize listed on website.

7 or more right, earn one grand prize entry per rules on website.

Details, official rules at ProFootballBeast.com

ProFootballBeast Prop Game For Week 9

1) Who wins, GB or CAR?	GB	CAR
2) Total Passing Yards for MIN?	<239.5	>239.5
3) Total points in OAK/PIT game?	<43.5	>43.5
4) Top Fantasy QB on Sun/Mon?	_____	
5) Who wins, NYG or TB?	NYG	TB
6) Total penalties in MIA/BUF game?	0	>0
7) Total # INTs in DEN/IND game?	<2.5	>2.5
8) Highest Scoring Team on Sun/Mon?	_____	
9) Total Yards for DAL?	<399.5	>399.5
10) Who wins, CHI or SD?	CHI	SD

EXTRAS:

Bold prediction of the week: _____

Best game day snack: _____

Friend you can throw a football farther than: _____

Link to winning entries must emailed to PFB for it to count. Full submission details at ProFootballBeast.com/weeklygame/
Want to play? Get yourself a copy ---> **GetTheBeastBook.com**

YOUR POWER POLL

Fill in your rankings, snap a picture, and share on social this week. Use the hashtag: #PFBPowerPoll

WEEK 9 NOTES:

_____
_____
_____
_____
_____
_____

MY NFL POWER POLL FOR WEEK 9

TOP 5 TEAMS   BOTTOM 5 TEAMS
1. _____   32. _____
2. _____   31. _____
3. _____   30. _____
4. _____   29. _____
5. _____   28. _____

YOUR TOP 3 MVP CANDIDATES RIGHT NOW
1. _____
2. _____
3. _____

To share your own power poll, get the book!
----------> **GetTheBeastBook.com** <----------

WEEK 10 (Nov 12th - Nov 16th)

Record results, the betting line, your picks, and home/road/fave/dog trends.
Or if this is too intense for you, just use it for schedule/scores.

WEEK 10 SCHEDULE / RESULTS

BYE: ATL, IND, SD, SF

ROAD	SCORE	HOME	LINE	MY PICK	W / L	H/R/F/D	TIME (ET)	TV
BUF	-	NYJ				HF HD RF RD	THU 8:25 PM	NFL
DET	-	GB				HF HD RF RD	SUN 1:00PM	FOX
DAL	-	TB				HF HD RF RD	SUN 1:00PM	FOX
CAR	-	TEN				HF HD RF RD	SUN 1:00PM	FOX
CHI	-	STL				HF HD RF RD	SUN 1:00PM	FOX
NO	-	WAS				HF HD RF RD	SUN 1:00PM	FOX
MIA	-	PHL				HF HD RF RD	SUN 1:00PM	CBS
CLE	-	PIT				HF HD RF RD	SUN 1:00PM	CBS
JAX	-	BAL				HF HD RF RD	SUN 1:00PM	CBS
MIN	-	OAK				HF HD RF RD	SUN 4:05PM	FOX
NE	-	NYG				HF HD RF RD	SUN 4:25PM	CBS
KC	-	DEN				HF HD RF RD	SUN 4:25PM	CBS
ARI	-	SEA				HF HD RF RD	SUN 8:30PM	NBC
HOU	-	CIN				HF HD RF RD	MON 8:30PM	ESPN
SUN GAMES MAY BE FLEXED TO 8:30			**TOTALS**					

ProFootballBeast Trash Talk Mad Libs

Hey _____, nice team you got there! I'd rather start _____ or a _____ on my team than start _____. Too bad our league doesn't give points for looking like an ugly _____, because your face would be undefeated. I hope _____'s _____ explodes during the national anthem. Get ready to lose by _____ points. Sincerely, _____

Want to share your own trash talk mad libs?
---------> GetTheBeastBook.com <-----------

FANTASY TRASH TALK MAD LIBS

Fill in the blanks then post a picture of it on FB, Twitter, or IG. Tag your opponent and use hashtag #PFBTrashTalk.
(We'll highlight best ones each week.)

Help for the 9 blanks to fill in:
1: Fantasy Owner you're facing this wk
2: a celebrity older than 55
3: any inanimate object
4: worst guy on your opponent's team
5: an animal your opponent looks like
6: a stud on your opponent's team
7: a body part
8: a number between 200-300
9: You (or your fantasy team name)

WEEKLY GAME

Complete, then snap a picture & share on FB, IG, or Twitter. Hashtag: #PFBPropGame

Entry must be posted: Between Thurs. 11/12 & Sun. 11/15 by 9am. (Eastern Time)

All 10 right, win prize listed on website.

7 or more right, earn one grand prize entry per rules on website.

Details, official rules at ProFootballBeast.com

ProFootballBeast Prop Game For Week 10

1) Who wins, CHI or STL?	CHI	STL
2) Largest lead in NO/WAS game	<14.5	>14.5
3) Total points in JAX/BAL game?	<44.5	>44.5
4) Name 1 of Top 2 fantasy RBs on Sun/Mon?	_____	
5) Who wins, NE or NYG?	NE	NYG
6) Total Rushing Yards for GB?	<109.5	>109.5
7) Total goals by Messi in MIN/OAK game?	0	>0
8) Highest Scoring Team on Sun/Mon?	_____	
9) Total Yards for ARI?	<319.5	>319.5
10) Who wins, HOU or CIN?	HOU	CIN

EXTRAS:

Bold prediction of the week: _____

Celeb you want to play you in a movie: _____

Favorite sport to watch besides football: _____

Link to winning entries must emailed to PFB for it to count. Full submission details at ProFootballBeast.com/weeklygame/
Want to play? Get yourself a copy ---> **GetTheBeastBook.com**

YOUR POWER POLL

Fill in your rankings, snap a picture, and share on social this week. Use the hashtag: #PFBPowerPoll

WEEK 10 NOTES:

_____
_____
_____
_____
_____
_____
_____

MY NFL POWER POLL FOR WEEK 10

TOP 5 TEAMS   BOTTOM 5 TEAMS
1._____   32._____
2._____   31._____
3._____   30._____
4._____   29._____
5._____   28._____

YOUR TOP 3 MOVIES YOU'VE SEEN THIS YEAR

1._____
2._____
3._____

To share your own power poll, get the book!
-------------> **GetTheBeastBook.com** <---------------

WEEK 11 (Nov 19th - Nov 23rd)

Record results, the betting line, your picks, and home/road/fave/dog trends.
Or if this is too intense for you, just use it for schedule/scores.

WEEK 11 SCHEDULE / RESULTS

BYE: CLE, NO, NYG, PIT

ROAD	SCORE	HOME	LINE	MY PICK	W/L	H/R/F/D	TIME (ET)	TV
TEN	-	JAX				HF HD RF RD	THU 8:25 PM	NFL
OAK	-	DET				HF HD RF RD	SUN 1:00PM	CBS
IND	-	ATL				HF HD RF RD	SUN 1:00PM	CBS
NYJ	-	HOU				HF HD RF RD	SUN 1:00PM	CBS
TB	-	PHL				HF HD RF RD	SUN 1:00PM	FOX
DEN	-	CHI				HF HD RF RD	SUN 1:00PM	CBS
GB	-	MIN				HF HD RF RD	SUN 1:00PM	FOX
STL	-	BAL				HF HD RF RD	SUN 1:00PM	FOX
DAL	-	MIA				HF HD RF RD	SUN 1:00PM	FOX
WAS	-	CAR				HF HD RF RD	SUN 1:00PM	FOX
CIN	-	ARI				HF HD RF RD	SUN 4:05PM	CBS
SF	-	SEA				HF HD RF RD	SUN 4:25PM	FOX
KC	-	SD				HF HD RF RD	SUN 8:30PM	NBC
BUF	-	NE				HF HD RF RD	MON 8:30PM	ESPN
SUN GAMES MAY BE FLEXED TO 8:30				**TOTALS**				

ProFootballBeast Trash Talk Mad Libs

Hey _____, I'm going to rip out your team's _____ and smash it to pieces with a _____ this week. _____ is going to make you beg for mercy. Your team smells like _____ mixed with _____ feces. I'd rather never play fantasy again than have your roster. Why _____, was _____ not available? May you never win a game again in this or any season, _____.

Want to share your own trash talk mad libs?
----------> **GetTheBeastBook.com** <------------

FANTASY TRASH TALK MAD LIBS
Fill in the blanks then post a picture of it on FB, Twitter, or IG. Tag your opponent and use hashtag #PFBTrashTalk.
(We'll highlight best ones each week.)

Help for the 9 blanks to fill in:
1: Fantasy Owner you're facing this wk
2: internal organ
3: any object
4: one of your best players
5: something gross
6: an animal
7: your opponent's worst player
8: retired player from the 80s or 90s
9: You (or your fantasy team name)

WEEKLY GAME

Complete, then snap a picture & share on FB, IG, or Twitter. Hashtag: #PFBPropGame

Entry must be posted: Between Thurs. 11/19 & Sun. 11/22 by 9am. (Eastern Time)

All 10 right, win prize listed on website.

7 or more right, earn one grand prize entry per rules on website.

Details, official rules at ProFootballBeast.com

ProFootballBeast Prop Game For Week 11

1) Who wins, NYJ or HOU?	NYJ	HOU
2) Total Von Miller farts during DEN/CHI?	<1500	>1500
3) Total points in IND/ATL game?	<54.5	>54.5
4) Top Fantasy QB on Sun/Mon?	_____	
5) Who wins, CIN or ARI?	CIN	ARI
6) Longest FG in ATL/BAL game?	<38.5	>38.5
7) Total # INTs in DAL/MIA game?	<2.5	>2.5
8) Highest Scoring Team on Sun/Mon?	_____	
9) Points scored in 4th Q of SF/SEA?	<13.5	>13.5
10) Who wins, KC or SD?	KC	SD

EXTRAS:
Bold prediction of the week: _____
Luckiest fantasy player in your league this yr: _____
Player you wish you didn't draft this yr: _____

Link to winning entries must emailed to PFB for it to count.
Full submission details at ProFootballBeast.com/weeklygame/
Want to play? Get yourself a copy ---> **GetTheBeastBook.com**

YOUR POWER POLL

Fill in your rankings, snap a picture, and share on social this week. Use the hashtag: #PFBPowerPoll

WEEK 11 NOTES:

_____
_____
_____
_____
_____
_____
_____

MY NFL POWER POLL FOR WEEK 11

TOP 5 TEAMS   BOTTOM 5 TEAMS
1. _____   32. _____
2. _____   31. _____
3. _____   30. _____
4. _____   29. _____
5. _____   28. _____

YOUR TOP 3 RUNNING BACK RANKINGS
1. _____
2. _____
3. _____

To share your own power poll, get the book!
-----------> **GetTheBeastBook.com** <-----------

WEEK 12 (Nov 26th - Nov 30th)

Record results, the betting line, your picks, and home/road/fave/dog trends.
Or if this is too intense for you, just use it for schedule/scores.

| \multicolumn{10}{c|}{WEEK 12 SCHEDULE / RESULTS} |
ROAD	SCORE	HOME	LINE	MY PICK	W / L	H/R/F/D	TIME (ET)	TV
PHL	-	DET				HF HD RF RD	THU 12:30PM	FOX
CAR	-	DAL				HF HD RF RD	THU 4:30PM	CBS
CHI	-	GB				HF HD RF RD	THU 8:30PM	NBC
OAK	-	TEN				HF HD RF RD	SUN 1:00PM	CBS
BUF	-	KC				HF HD RF RD	SUN 1:00PM	CBS
TB	-	IND				HF HD RF RD	SUN 1:00PM	FOX
NYG	-	WAS				HF HD RF RD	SUN 1:00PM	FOX
NO	-	HOU				HF HD RF RD	SUN 1:00PM	FOX
MIN	-	ATL				HF HD RF RD	SUN 1:00PM	FOX
STL	-	CIN				HF HD RF RD	SUN 1:00PM	FOX
SD	-	JAX				HF HD RF RD	SUN 1:00PM	CBS
MIA	-	NYJ				HF HD RF RD	SUN 1:00PM	CBS
ARI	-	SF				HF HD RF RD	SUN 4:05PM	FOX
PIT	-	SEA				HF HD RF RD	SUN 4:25PM	CBS
NE	-	DEN				HF HD RF RD	SUN 8:30PM	NBC
BAL	-	CLE				HF HD RF RD	MON 8:30PM	ESPN
SUN GAMES MAY BE FLEXED TO 8:30				TOTALS				

ProFootballBeast Trash Talk Mad Libs

Hey _____, get ready to hate _____ because he's going to smash you in the _____ with a bag of _____ all day. Why is _____ on your roster? You know we don't get points for injuries, right? I hope _____ gets mauled by an escaped _____ during the coin toss. Remember when you drafted _____? That's when I knew you sucked. Worst of luck, _____.

Want to share your own trash talk mad libs?
----------> GetTheBeastBook.com <------------

FANTASY TRASH TALK MAD LIBS
Fill in the blanks then post a picture of it on FB, Twitter, or IG. Tag your opponent and use hashtag #PFBTrashTalk.
(We'll highlight best ones each week.)

Help for the 9 blanks to fill in:
1: Fantasy Owner you're facing this wk
2: your best player this week
3: body part
4: random object (plural)
5: injured guy on roster (or injury prone)
6: your opponent's best player
7: zoo animal
8: opponent's worst pick (research it)
9: You (or your fantasy team name)

WEEKLY GAME

Complete, then snap a picture & share on FB, IG, or Twitter. Hashtag: #PFBPropGame

Entry must be posted: Between Thurs. 11/26 & Sun. 11/29 by 9am. (Eastern Time)

All 10 right, win prize listed on website.

7 or more right, earn one grand prize entry per rules on website.

Details, official rules at ProFootballBeast.com

ProFootballBeast Prop Game For Week 12

1) Who wins, OAK or TEN?	OAK	TEN
2) Longest TD in TB/IND game?	<39.5	>39.5
3) Total points in MIA/NYJ game?	<44.5	>44.5
4) Name 1 of Top 3 fantasy WRs on Sun/Mon?	_____	
5) Who wins, NO or HOU?	NO	HOU
6) Total Yards for OAK?	<319.5	>319.5
7) Total Miyagi crane kicks during STL/CIN?	0	>0
8) Highest Scoring Team on Sun/Mon?	_____	
9) Total made FGs in BAL/CLE game?	<3.5	>3.5
10) Who wins, NE or DEN?	NE	DEN

EXTRAS:

Bold prediction of the week: _____

Turkey: white meat, dark meat, or no meat: _____

Best Thanksgiving meal side dish: _____

*Link to winning entries must emailed to PFB for it to count. Full submission details at ProFootballBeast.com/weeklygame/ Want to play? Get yourself a copy ---> **GetTheBeastBook.com***

YOUR POWER POLL

Fill in your rankings, snap a picture, and share on social this week. Use the hashtag: #PFBPowerPoll

WEEK 12 NOTES:

_____
_____
_____
_____
_____
_____

MY NFL POWER POLL FOR WEEK 12

TOP 5 TEAMS   BOTTOM 5 TEAMS

1._____   32._____
2._____   31._____
3._____   30._____
4._____   29._____
5._____   28._____

TOP 3 THANKSGIVING DINNER SIDE DISHES

1._____
2._____
3._____

To share your own power poll, get the book!
-------------> **GetTheBeastBook.com** <-------------

WEEK 13 (Dec 3rd - Dec 7th)

Record results, the betting line, your picks, and home/road/fave/dog trends.
Or if this is too intense for you, just use it for schedule/scores.

WEEK 13 SCHEDULE / RESULTS

ROAD	SCORE	HOME	LINE	MY PICK	W / L	H/R/F/D	TIME (ET)	TV
GB	-	DET				HF HD RF RD	THU 8:25PM	CBS
NYJ	-	NYG				HF HD RF RD	SUN 1:00PM	CBS
ARI	-	STL				HF HD RF RD	SUN 1:00PM	FOX
ATL	-	TB				HF HD RF RD	SUN 1:00PM	FOX
CAR	-	NO				HF HD RF RD	SUN 1:00PM	FOX
SEA	-	MIN				HF HD RF RD	SUN 1:00PM	FOX
HOU	-	BUF				HF HD RF RD	SUN 1:00PM	CBS
BAL	-	MIA				HF HD RF RD	SUN 1:00PM	CBS
CIN	-	CLE				HF HD RF RD	SUN 1:00PM	CBS
JAX	-	TEN				HF HD RF RD	SUN 1:00PM	CBS
SF	-	CHI				HF HD RF RD	SUN 1:00PM	FOX
DEN	-	SD				HF HD RF RD	SUN 4:05PM	CBS
KC	-	OAK				HF HD RF RD	SUN 4:05PM	CBS
PHL	-	NE				HF HD RF RD	SUN 4:25PM	FOX
IND	-	PIT				HF HD RF RD	SUN 8:30PM	NBC
DAL	-	WAS				HF HD RF RD	MON 8:30PM	ESPN
SUN GAMES MAY BE FLEXED TO 8:30				TOTALS				

ProFootballBeast Trash Talk Mad Libs

Hey _____, I'm going to rip out your team's heart and smash it to pieces with a _____ this week. I hope a _____ falls on _____ during the pre-game and _____'s arm turns into a _____ in the 2nd quarter. You won't win one more game this year. I'd rather eat _____ covered in _____ than have your players. Worst of luck this week, _____.

Want to share your own trash talk mad libs?
----------> GetTheBeastBook.com <----------

FANTASY TRASH TALK MAD LIBS

Fill in the blanks then post a picture of it on FB, Twitter, or IG. Tag your opponent and use hashtag #PFBTrashTalk.
(We'll highlight best ones each week.)

Help for the 9 blanks to fill in:
1: Fantasy Owner you're facing this wk
2: a tool or weapon
3: a heavy object
4: an opposing fantasy WR
5: the opposing fantasy QB
6: a random object
7: something nasty
8: another something nasty
9: You (or your fantasy team name)

WEEKLY GAME

Complete, then snap a picture & share on FB, IG, or Twitter. Hashtag: #PFBPropGame

Entry must be posted: Between Thurs. 12/3 & Sun. 12/6 by 9am. (Eastern Time)

All 10 right, win prize listed on website.

7 or more right, earn one grand prize entry per rules on website.

Details, official rules at ProFootballBeast.com

ProFootballBeast Prop Game For Week 13

1) Who wins, NYJ or NYG?	NYJ	NYG
2) Longest passing TD in CAR/NO game?	<29.5	>29.5
3) Total points in HOU/BUF game?	<43.5	>43.5
4) Top Fantasy QB on Sun/Mon?	_____	
5) Who wins, SEA or MIN?	SEA	MIN
6) Total sideline unicorns in BAL/MIA game?	0	>0
7) Total # INTs in DEN/SD game?	<2.5	>2.5
8) Highest Scoring Team on Sun/Mon?	_____	
9) Total Yards for DAL?	<399.5	>399.5
10) Who wins, IND or PIT?	IND	PIT

EXTRAS:
Bold prediction of the week: _____
Worst fantasy player on your current roster: _____
Friend who couldn't even kick a 20-yd FG: _____

Link to winning entries must emailed to PFB for it to count. Full submission details at ProFootballBeast.com/weeklygame/
Want to play? Get yourself a copy ---> **GetTheBeastBook.com**

YOUR POWER POLL

Fill in your rankings, snap a picture, and share on social this week. Use the hashtag: #PFBPowerPoll

WEEK 13 NOTES:

_____
_____
_____
_____
_____
_____
_____

MY NFL POWER POLL FOR WEEK 13

TOP 5 TEAMS	BOTTOM 5 TEAMS
1._____	32._____
2._____	31._____
3._____	30._____
4._____	29._____
5._____	28._____

WHO'S IN YOUR TOP 4 FOR THE COLLEGE FOOTBALL PLAYOFF?

1._____   3._____
2._____   4._____

To share your own power poll, get the book!
-----------> **GetTheBeastBook.com** <-----------

WEEK 14 (Dec 10th - Dec 14th)

Record results, the betting line, your picks, and home/road/fave/dog trends.
Or if this is too intense for you, just use it for schedule/scores.

WEEK 14 SCHEDULE / RESULTS

ROAD	SCORE	HOME	LINE	MY PICK	W/L	H/R/F/D	TIME (ET)	TV
MIN	-	ARI				HF HD RF RD	THU 8:25PM	NFL
BUF	-	PHL				HF HD RF RD	SUN 1:00PM	CBS
SF	-	CLE				HF HD RF RD	SUN 1:00PM	FOX
DET	-	STL				HF HD RF RD	SUN 1:00PM	FOX
NO	-	TB				HF HD RF RD	SUN 1:00PM	FOX
TEN	-	NYJ				HF HD RF RD	SUN 1:00PM	CBS
PIT	-	CIN				HF HD RF RD	SUN 1:00PM	CBS
NE	-	HOU				HF HD RF RD	SUN 1:00PM	CBS
IND	-	JAX				HF HD RF RD	SUN 1:00PM	CBS
SD	-	KC				HF HD RF RD	SUN 1:00PM	CBS
WAS	-	CHI				HF HD RF RD	SUN 1:00PM	FOX
ATL	-	CAR				HF HD RF RD	SUN 1:00PM	FOX
OAK	-	DEN				HF HD RF RD	SUN 4:05PM	CBS
DAL	-	GB				HF HD RF RD	SUN 4:25PM	FOX
SEA	-	BAL				HF HD RF RD	SUN 8:30PM	NBC
NYG	-	MIA				HF HD RF RD	MON 8:30PM	ESPN
SUN GAMES MAY BE FLEXED TO 8:30				TOTALS				

ProFootballBeast Trash Talk Mad Libs

Hey _____, nice team you got there! I'd rather start _____ or a _____ on my team than start _____. Too bad our league doesn't give points for looking like a shriveled _____, because your face would never lose. I hope _____'s _____ explodes during the opening kickoff. Get ready to lose by _____ points. Sincerely, _____

Want to share your own trash trash talk mad libs?
---------> **GetTheBeastBook.com** <-----------

FANTASY TRASH TALK MAD LIBS
Fill in the blanks then post a picture of it on FB, Twitter, or IG. Tag your opponent and use hashtag #PFBTrashTalk.
(We'll highlight best ones each week.)

Help for the 9 blanks to fill in:
1: Fantasy Owner you're facing this wk
2: a fantasy owner in your league
3: any inanimate object
4: worst guy on your opponent's team
5: an animal your opponent looks like
6: a stud on your opponent's team
7: a body part
8: a number between 150-250
9: You (or your fantasy team name)

WEEKLY GAME

Complete, then snap a picture & share on FB, IG, or Twitter. Hashtag: #PFBPropGame

Entry must be posted: Between Thurs. 12/10 & Sun. 12/13 by 9am. (Eastern Time)

All 10 right, win prize listed on website.

7 or more right, earn one grand prize entry per rules on website.

Details, official rules at ProFootballBeast.com

ProFootballBeast Prop Game For Week 14

1) Who wins, ATL or CAR?	ATL	CAR
2) Largest lead in BUF/PHL game	<14.5	>14.5
3) Total goaltending calls during NO/TB?	0	>0
4) Name 1 of Top 2 fantasy RBs on Sun/Mon?	_____	
5) Who wins, SD or KC?	SD	KC
6) Total Rushing Yards for NYJ?	<139.5	>139.5
7) Total # INTs in SF/CLE game?	<3.5	>3.5
8) Highest Scoring Team on Sun/Mon?	_____	
9) Total Yards for GB?	<399.5	>399.5
10) Who wins, SEA or BAL?	SEA	BAL

EXTRAS:
Bold prediction of the week: _____
How many fantasy leagues are you in: _____
In how many leagues are you in playoffs: _____

Link to winning entries must emailed to PFB for it to count. Full submission details at ProFootballBeast.com/weeklygame/
Want to play? Get yourself a copy ---> **GetTheBeastBook.com**

YOUR POWER POLL

Fill in your rankings, snap a picture, and share on social this week. Use the hashtag: #PFBPowerPoll

WEEK 14 NOTES:

_____
_____
_____
_____
_____
_____
_____

MY NFL POWER POLL FOR WEEK 14

TOP 5 TEAMS	BOTTOM 5 TEAMS
1._____	32._____
2._____	31._____
3._____	30._____
4._____	29._____
5._____	28._____

YOUR TOP 3 MVP CANDIDATES RIGHT NOW

1._____
2._____
3._____

To share your own power poll, get the book!
--------------> **GetTheBeastBook.com** <--------------

WEEK 15 (Dec 17th - Dec 21st)

Record results, the betting line, your picks, and home/road/fave/dog trends.
Or if this is too intense for you, just use it for schedule/scores.

WEEK 15 SCHEDULE / RESULTS

ROAD	SCORE	HOME	LINE	MY PICK	W/L	H/R/F/D	TIME (ET)	TV
TB	-	STL				HF HD RF RD	THU 8:25PM	NFL
NYJ	-	DAL				HF HD RF RD	SAT 8:25PM	NFL
CHI	-	MIN				HF HD RF RD	SUN 1:00PM	FOX
ATL	-	JAX				HF HD RF RD	SUN 1:00PM	FOX
HOU	-	IND				HF HD RF RD	SUN 1:00PM	CBS
ARI	-	PHL				HF HD RF RD	SUN 1:00PM	FOX
CAR	-	NYG				HF HD RF RD	SUN 1:00PM	FOX
TEN	-	NE				HF HD RF RD	SUN 1:00PM	CBS
BUF	-	WAS				HF HD RF RD	SUN 1:00PM	CBS
KC	-	BAL				HF HD RF RD	SUN 1:00PM	CBS
CLE	-	SEA				HF HD RF RD	SUN 4:05PM	FOX
GB	-	OAK				HF HD RF RD	SUN 4:05PM	FOX
DEN	-	PIT				HF HD RF RD	SUN 4:25PM	CBS
MIA	-	SD				HF HD RF RD	SUN 4:25PM	CBS
CIN	-	SF				HF HD RF RD	SUN 8:30PM	NBC
DET	-	NO				HF HD RF RD	MON 8:30PM	ESPN
SUN GAMES MAY BE FLEXED TO 8:30				TOTALS				

ProFootballBeast Trash Talk Mad Libs

Hey _____, I'm going to rip out your team's _____ and smash it to pieces with a _____ this week. _____ is going to make you beg for mercy. Your team smells like _____ mixed with _____ turds. I'd rather never play fantasy again than have your roster. Why _____, was _____ not available? May you never win a game again in this or any season, _____.

Want to share your own trash talk mad libs?
----------> GetTheBeastBook.com <----------

FANTASY TRASH TALK MAD LIBS

Fill in the blanks then post a picture of it on FB, Twitter, or IG. Tag your opponent and use hashtag #PFBTrashTalk.
(We'll highlight best ones each week.)

Help for the 9 blanks to fill in:
1: Fantasy Owner you're facing this wk
2: internal organ
3: any object
4: one of your best players
5: something gross
6: an animal
7: your opponent's worst player
8: retired player from the 80s or 90s
9: You (or your fantasy team name)

WEEKLY GAME

Complete, then snap a picture & share on FB, IG, or Twitter. Hashtag: #PFBPropGame

Entry must be posted: Between Thurs. 12/17 & Sun. 12/20 by 9am. (Eastern Time)

All 10 right, win prize listed on website.

7 or more right, earn one grand prize entry per rules on website.

Details, official rules at ProFootballBeast.com

ProFootballBeast Prop Game For Week 15

1) Who wins, ARI or PHL?	ARI	PHL
2) Total Rushing Yards for MIN?	<114.5	>114.5
3) Total points in CAR/NYG game?	<45.5	>45.5
4) Top Fantasy QB on Sun/Mon?	_____	
5) Who wins, KC or BAL?	KC	BAL
6) Longest FG in BUF/WAS game?	<34.5	>34.5
7) Total fires started on PIT 50-yard line?	0	>0
8) Highest Scoring Team on Sun/Mon?	_____	
9) Points scored in 1st Q of CIN/SF?	<13.5	>13.5
10) Who wins, DET or NO?	DET	NO

EXTRAS:

Bold prediction of the week: _____

How many fantasy leagues are you still alive in: _____

Luckiest fantasy owner still alive in playoffs: _____

Link to winning entries must emailed to PFB for it to count. Full submission details at ProFootballBeast.com/weeklygame/
Want to play? Get yourself a copy ---> **GetTheBeastBook.com**

YOUR POWER POLL

Fill in your rankings, snap a picture, and share on social this week. Use the hashtag: #PFBPowerPoll

WEEK 15 NOTES:

_____
_____
_____
_____
_____
_____
_____

MY NFL POWER POLL FOR WEEK 15

TOP 5 TEAMS   BOTTOM 5 TEAMS

1. _____   32. _____
2. _____   31. _____
3. _____   30. _____
4. _____   29. _____
5. _____   28. _____

YOUR TOP 3 MOST OVERRATED HOLIDAYS

1. _____
2. _____
3. _____

To share your own power poll, get the book!
----------------> **GetTheBeastBook.com** <----------------

WEEK 16 (Dec 24th - Dec 28th)

Record results, the betting line, your picks, and home/road/fave/dog trends.
Or if this is too intense for you, just use it for schedule/scores.

WEEK 16 SCHEDULE / RESULTS

ROAD	SCORE	HOME	LINE	MY PICK	W/L	H/R/F/D	TIME (ET)	TV
SD	-	OAK				HF HD RF RD	THU 8:25PM	NFL
WAS	-	PHL				HF HD RF RD	SAT 8:25PM	NFL
NE	-	NYJ				HF HD RF RD	SUN 1:00PM	CBS
HOU	-	TEN				HF HD RF RD	SUN 1:00PM	CBS
CLE	-	KC				HF HD RF RD	SUN 1:00PM	CBS
IND	-	MIA				HF HD RF RD	SUN 1:00PM	CBS
JAX	-	NO				HF HD RF RD	SUN 1:00PM	CBS
SF	-	DET				HF HD RF RD	SUN 1:00PM	FOX
DAL	-	BUF				HF HD RF RD	SUN 1:00PM	FOX
CHI	-	TB				HF HD RF RD	SUN 1:00PM	FOX
CAR	-	ATL				HF HD RF RD	SUN 1:00PM	FOX
NYG	-	MIN				HF HD RF RD	SUN 1:00PM	FOX
STL	-	SEA				HF HD RF RD	SUN 4:25PM	FOX
GB	-	ARI				HF HD RF RD	SUN 4:25PM	FOX
PIT	-	BAL				HF HD RF RD	SUN 8:30PM	NBC
CIN	-	DEN				HF HD RF RD	MON 8:30PM	ESPN
SUN GAMES MAY BE FLEXED TO 8:30				TOTALS				

ProFootballBeast Trash Talk Mad Libs

Hey _____, get ready to hate _____ because he's going to smash you in the _____ with a bag of _____ all day. Why is _____ on your roster? You know we don't get points for injuries, right? I hope _____ gets eaten by a rabid _____ during the coin toss. Remember when you drafted _____? That's when I knew you sucked. Worst of luck, _____.

Want to share your own trash talk mad libs? It's Week 16, dude. Get 'em next year.

FANTASY TRASH TALK MAD LIBS

Fill in the blanks then post a picture of it on FB, Twitter, or IG. Tag your opponent and use hashtag #PFBTrashTalk. (We'll highlight best ones each week.)

Help for the 9 blanks to fill in:
1: Fantasy Owner you're facing this wk
2: your best player this week
3: body part
4: random object (plural)
5: injured guy on roster (or injury prone)
6: your opponent's best player
7: wild animal
8: opponent's worst pick (research it)
9: You (or your fantasy team name)

WEEKLY GAME

Complete, then snap a picture & share on FB, IG, or Twitter. Hashtag: #PFBPropGame

Entry must be posted: Between Thurs. 12/24 & Sun. 12/27 by 9am. (Eastern Time)

All 10 right, win prize listed on website.

7 or more right, earn one grand prize entry per rules on website.

Details, official rules at ProFootballBeast.com

ProFootballBeast Prop Game For Week 16

1) Who wins, HOU or TEN? HOU TEN
2) Longest TD in NE/NYJ game? <39.5 >39.5
3) Total points in CHI/TB game? <40.5 >40.5
4) Name 1 of Top 3 fantasy WRs on Sun/Mon? _____
5) Who wins, DAL or BUF? DAL BUF
6) Total player trades during CLE/KC game? 0 >0
7) Total Kickoff return TDs on Sunday? <0.5 >0.5
8) Highest Scoring Team on Sun/Mon? _____
9) Total made FGs in GB/ARI game? <3.5 >3.5
10) Who wins, PIT or BAL? PIT BAL

EXTRAS:
Bold prediction of the week: _____
Best Christmas gift you got this yr: _____
Still alive in any fantasy leagues: _____

Link to winning entries must emailed to PFB for it to count. Full submission details at ProFootballBeast.com/weeklygame/
Want to play? It's Week 16, dude. Get 'em next year.

YOUR POWER POLL

Fill in your rankings, snap a picture, and share on social this week. Use the hashtag: #PFBPowerPoll

WEEK 16 NOTES:

_____
_____
_____
_____
_____
_____
_____

MY NFL POWER POLL FOR WEEK 16

TOP 5 TEAMS   BOTTOM 5 TEAMS
1._____   32._____
2._____   31._____
3._____   30._____
4._____   29._____
5._____   28._____

YOUR 3 LEAST FAVORITE CHRISTMAS SONGS
1._____
2._____
3._____

Want to play?
It's Week 16, dude. Get 'em next year.

WEEK 17 (January 3, 2016)

Record results, the betting line, your picks, and home/road/fave/dog trends.
Or if this is too intense for you, just use it for schedule/scores.

WEEK 17 SCHEDULE / RESULTS

ROAD	SCORE	HOME	LINE	MY PICK	W/L	H/R/F/D	TIME (ET)	TV
NYJ	-	BUF				HF HD RF RD	SUN 1:00PM	CBS
NE	-	MIA				HF HD RF RD	SUN 1:00PM	CBS
TB	-	CAR				HF HD RF RD	SUN 1:00PM	FOX
NO	-	ATL				HF HD RF RD	SUN 1:00PM	FOX
BAL	-	CIN				HF HD RF RD	SUN 1:00PM	CBS
PIT	-	CLE				HF HD RF RD	SUN 1:00PM	CBS
JAX	-	HOU				HF HD RF RD	SUN 1:00PM	CBS
TEN	-	IND				HF HD RF RD	SUN 1:00PM	CBS
OAK	-	KC				HF HD RF RD	SUN 1:00PM	CBS
WAS	-	DAL				HF HD RF RD	SUN 1:00PM	FOX
PHL	-	NYG				HF HD RF RD	SUN 1:00PM	FOX
DET	-	CHI				HF HD RF RD	SUN 1:00PM	FOX
MIN	-	GB				HF HD RF RD	SUN 1:00PM	FOX
SD	-	DEN				HF HD RF RD	SUN 4:25PM	CBS
SEA	-	ARI				HF HD RF RD	SUN 4:25PM	FOX
STL	-	SF				HF HD RF RD	SUN 4:25PM	FOX
SUN GAMES MAY BE FLEXED TO 8:30				TOTALS				

ProFootballBeast Trash Talk Mad Libs

Hey _____, I'm going to rip out your team's heart and smash it to pieces with a _____ this week. I hope a _____ falls on _____ during the pre-game and _____'s arm turns into a _____ in the 1st quarter. You will never get this lucky in fantasy again. I'd rather eat _____ covered in _____ than have your players. Worst of luck this week, _____.

Want to share your own trash talk mad libs? It's Week 17, bro. You waited too long.

FANTASY TRASH TALK MAD LIBS

Fill in the blanks then post a picture of it on FB, Twitter, or IG. Tag your opponent and use hashtag #PFBTrashTalk. *(We'll highlight best ones each week.)*

Help for the 9 blanks to fill in:
1: Fantasy Owner you're facing this wk
2: a tool or weapon
3: a heavy object
4: an opposing fantasy WR
5: the opposing fantasy QB
6: a random object
7: something nasty
8: another something nasty
9: You (or your fantasy team name)

WEEKLY GAME

Complete, then snap a picture & share on FB, IG, or Twitter. Hashtag: #PFBPropGame

Entry must be posted: Between Thurs. 12/31 & Sun. 1/3/16 by 9am. (Eastern Time)

All 10 right, win prize listed on website.

7 or more right, earn one grand prize entry per rules on website.

Details, official rules at ProFootballBeast.com

ProFootballBeast Prop Game For Week 17

1) Who wins, NYJ or BUF?	NYJ	BUF
2) Longest passing TD in NE/MIA game?	<29.5	>29.5
3) Total on-field llamas during BAL/CIN?	0	>0
4) Top Fantasy QB on Sun/Mon?	_____	
5) Longest made FG in OAK/KC game?	<35.5	>35.5
6) Total Rushing Yards for GB?	<119.5	>119.5
7) Total # INTs in WAS/DAL game?	<3.5	>3.5
8) Highest Scoring Team on Sun/Mon?	_____	
9) Total Yards for ARI?	<369.5	>369.5
10) Who wins, STL or SF?	STL	SF

EXTRAS:
Bold prediction of the week: _____
Did you win any fantasy leagues: _____
Who should be kicked out of your league: _____

Link to winning entries must emailed to PFB for it to count. Full submission details at ProFootballBeast.com/weeklygame/
Want to play? It's Week 17, bro. You waited too long.

YOUR POWER POLL

Fill in your rankings, snap a picture, and share on social this week. Use the hashtag: #PFBPowerPoll

WEEK 17 NOTES:

_____
_____
_____
_____
_____
_____
_____

MY NFL POWER POLL FOR WEEK 17

TOP 5 TEAMS	BOTTOM 5 TEAMS
1._____	32._____
2._____	31._____
3._____	30._____
4._____	29._____
5._____	28._____

TOP 3 SB50 MATCH-UPS YOU WANT TO SEE
1._____
2._____
3._____

Want to share your own power poll?
It's Week 17, bro. You waited too long.

PART IV*
PREDICTIONS
(AND OTHER NONSENSE)

*The fourth part**

(it comes between parts III and V)*

***Hi.

MY 2015 NFL PLAYOFF PREDICTIONS

—

NFC SEEDS
1. _____
2. _____
3. _____
4. _____
5. _____
6. _____

AFC SEEDS
1. _____
2. _____
3. _____
4. _____
5. _____
6. _____

TOP 6 DRAFT PICKS
1. _____
2. _____
3. _____
4. _____
5. _____
6. _____

NFC PLAYOFFS
RD 1: _____
RD 1: _____
RD 2: _____
RD 2: _____
RD 3: _____

AFC PLAYOFFS
RD 1: _____
RD 1: _____
RD 2: _____
RD 2: _____
RD 3: _____

CHAMPIONSHIP GAME

_____

(fill out your predictions, take a picture, and share them on social before the season starts with the hashtag #PFBPicks)

MY 2015 NFL PLAYOFF PREDICTIONS

—

NFC SEEDS
1. Green Bay (12-4)
2. Seattle (11-5)
3. Dallas (10-6)
4. Atlanta (9-7)
5. Arizona (10-6)
6. Minnesota (10-6)

AFC SEEDS
1. Indianapolis (13-3)
2. Baltimore (10-6)
3. San Diego (10-6)
4. New England (10-6)
5. Denver (10-6)
6. Pittsburgh (9-7)

TOP 6 DRAFT PICKS
1. Tennessee (3-13)
2. Washington (3-13)
3. Cleveland (4-12)
4. Chicago (4-12)
5. Jacksonville (5-11)
6. Tampa Bay (5-11)

NFC PLAYOFFS
RD 1: **#3 DAL 34**, #6 MIN 31
RD 1: #4 ATL 21, **#5 ARI 28**
RD 2: **#1 GB 34**, #5 ARI 20
RD 2: **#2 SEA 28**, #3 DAL 27
RD 3: #1 GB 23, **#2 SEA 31**

AFC PLAYOFFS
RD 1: #3 SD 20, **#6 PIT 30**
RD 1: **#4 NE 38**, #5 DEN 24
RD 2: **#1 IND 41**, #6 PIT 31
RD 2: **#2 BAL 27**, #4 NE 21
RD 3: **#1 IND 34**, #2 BAL 30

CHAMPIONSHIP GAME

Seattle 34, Indianapolis 28

ADDITIONAL THOUGHTS: I don't feel great about having Atlanta in the playoffs, but you gotta make a bold prediction somewhere, so I'm doing that in the NFC South...I was leaning towards a GB-IND Super Bowl, but so many of my readers went that way that I had to go in a different direction...picking Seattle to win the NFC Championship in Lambeau is a little nuts, especially since it feels like the Packers should win the Lombardi in the 50th Super Bowl...I don't love the Colts defense, but I do love the home field advantage I expect them to have...I almost went with GB over BAL as my pick, but I'm sticking with Wilson over Luck.

WEEKLY KNOCKOUT/SUICIDE POOL TRACKER #1

1	2	3	4	5	6	7	8	9	10	11	12	13	14	15	16	17
DAL	DAL	DAL	DAL	DAL	DAL	DAL	DAL	DAL	DAL	DAL	DAL	DAL	DAL	DAL	DAL	DAL
PHL	PHL	PHL	PHL	PHL	PHL	PHL	PHL	PHL	PHL	PHL	PHL	PHL	PHL	PHL	PHL	PHL
NYG	NYG	NYG	NYG	NYG	NYG	NYG	NYG	NYG	NYG	NYG	NYG	NYG	NYG	NYG	NYG	NYG
WAS	WAS	WAS	WAS	WAS	WAS	WAS	WAS	WAS	WAS	WAS	WAS	WAS	WAS	WAS	WAS	WAS
GB	GB	GB	GB	GB	GB	GB	GB	GB	GB	GB	GB	GB	GB	GB	GB	GB
DET	DET	DET	DET	DET	DET	DET	DET	DET	DET	DET	DET	DET	DET	DET	DET	DET
MIN	MIN	MIN	MIN	MIN	MIN	MIN	MIN	MIN	MIN	MIN	MIN	MIN	MIN	MIN	MIN	MIN
CHI	CHI	CHI	CHI	CHI	CHI	CHI	CHI	CHI	CHI	CHI	CHI	CHI	CHI	CHI	CHI	CHI
ATL	ATL	ATL	ATL	ATL	ATL	ATL	ATL	ATL	ATL	ATL	ATL	ATL	ATL	ATL	ATL	ATL
CAR	CAR	CAR	CAR	CAR	CAR	CAR	CAR	CAR	CAR	CAR	CAR	CAR	CAR	CAR	CAR	CAR
TB	TB	TB	TB	TB	TB	TB	TB	TB	TB	TB	TB	TB	TB	TB	TB	TB
NO	NO	NO	NO	NO	NO	NO	NO	NO	NO	NO	NO	NO	NO	NO	NO	NO
SEA	SEA	SEA	SEA	SEA	SEA	SEA	SEA	SEA	SEA	SEA	SEA	SEA	SEA	SEA	SEA	SEA
SF	SF	SF	SF	SF	SF	SF	SF	SF	SF	SF	SF	SF	SF	SF	SF	SF
STL	STL	STL	STL	STL	STL	STL	STL	STL	STL	STL	STL	STL	STL	STL	STL	STL
ARI	ARI	ARI	ARI	ARI	ARI	ARI	ARI	ARI	ARI	ARI	ARI	ARI	ARI	ARI	ARI	ARI
NE	NE	NE	NE	NE	NE	NE	NE	NE	NE	NE	NE	NE	NE	NE	NE	NE
MIA	MIA	MIA	MIA	MIA	MIA	MIA	MIA	MIA	MIA	MIA	MIA	MIA	MIA	MIA	MIA	MIA
BUF	BUF	BUF	BUF	BUF	BUF	BUF	BUF	BUF	BUF	BUF	BUF	BUF	BUF	BUF	BUF	BUF
NYJ	NYJ	NYJ	NYJ	NYJ	NYJ	NYJ	NYJ	NYJ	NYJ	NYJ	NYJ	NYJ	NYJ	NYJ	NYJ	NYJ
CIN	CIN	CIN	CIN	CIN	CIN	CIN	CIN	CIN	CIN	CIN	CIN	CIN	CIN	CIN	CIN	CIN
PIT	PIT	PIT	PIT	PIT	PIT	PIT	PIT	PIT	PIT	PIT	PIT	PIT	PIT	PIT	PIT	PIT
CLE	CLE	CLE	CLE	CLE	CLE	CLE	CLE	CLE	CLE	CLE	CLE	CLE	CLE	CLE	CLE	CLE
BAL	BAL	BAL	BAL	BAL	BAL	BAL	BAL	BAL	BAL	BAL	BAL	BAL	BAL	BAL	BAL	BAL
HOU	HOU	HOU	HOU	HOU	HOU	HOU	HOU	HOU	HOU	HOU	HOU	HOU	HOU	HOU	HOU	HOU
IND	IND	IND	IND	IND	IND	IND	IND	IND	IND	IND	IND	IND	IND	IND	IND	IND
TEN	TEN	TEN	TEN	TEN	TEN	TEN	TEN	TEN	TEN	TEN	TEN	TEN	TEN	TEN	TEN	TEN
JAX	JAX	JAX	JAX	JAX	JAX	JAX	JAX	JAX	JAX	JAX	JAX	JAX	JAX	JAX	JAX	JAX
DEN	DEN	DEN	DEN	DEN	DEN	DEN	DEN	DEN	DEN	DEN	DEN	DEN	DEN	DEN	DEN	DEN
KC	KC	KC	KC	KC	KC	KC	KC	KC	KC	KC	KC	KC	KC	KC	KC	KC
SD	SD	SD	SD	SD	SD	SD	SD	SD	SD	SD	SD	SD	SD	SD	SD	SD
OAK	OAK	OAK	OAK	OAK	OAK	OAK	OAK	OAK	OAK	OAK	OAK	OAK	OAK	OAK	OAK	OAK

WEEKLY KNOCKOUT/SUICIDE POOL TRACKER #2

1	2	3	4	5	6	7	8	9	10	11	12	13	14	15	16	17
DAL	DAL	DAL	DAL	DAL	DAL	DAL	DAL	DAL	DAL	DAL	DAL	DAL	DAL	DAL	DAL	DAL
PHL	PHL	PHL	PHL	PHL	PHL	PHL	PHL	PHL	PHL	PHL	PHL	PHL	PHL	PHL	PHL	PHL
NYG	NYG	NYG	NYG	NYG	NYG	NYG	NYG	NYG	NYG	NYG	NYG	NYG	NYG	NYG	NYG	NYG
WAS	WAS	WAS	WAS	WAS	WAS	WAS	WAS	WAS	WAS	WAS	WAS	WAS	WAS	WAS	WAS	WAS
GB	GB	GB	GB	GB	GB	GB	GB	GB	GB	GB	GB	GB	GB	GB	GB	GB
DET	DET	DET	DET	DET	DET	DET	DET	DET	DET	DET	DET	DET	DET	DET	DET	DET
MIN	MIN	MIN	MIN	MIN	MIN	MIN	MIN	MIN	MIN	MIN	MIN	MIN	MIN	MIN	MIN	MIN
CHI	CHI	CHI	CHI	CHI	CHI	CHI	CHI	CHI	CHI	CHI	CHI	CHI	CHI	CHI	CHI	CHI
ATL	ATL	ATL	ATL	ATL	ATL	ATL	ATL	ATL	ATL	ATL	ATL	ATL	ATL	ATL	ATL	ATL
CAR	CAR	CAR	CAR	CAR	CAR	CAR	CAR	CAR	CAR	CAR	CAR	CAR	CAR	CAR	CAR	CAR
TB	TB	TB	TB	TB	TB	TB	TB	TB	TB	TB	TB	TB	TB	TB	TB	TB
NO	NO	NO	NO	NO	NO	NO	NO	NO	NO	NO	NO	NO	NO	NO	NO	NO
SEA	SEA	SEA	SEA	SEA	SEA	SEA	SEA	SEA	SEA	SEA	SEA	SEA	SEA	SEA	SEA	SEA
SF	SF	SF	SF	SF	SF	SF	SF	SF	SF	SF	SF	SF	SF	SF	SF	SF
STL	STL	STL	STL	STL	STL	STL	STL	STL	STL	STL	STL	STL	STL	STL	STL	STL
ARI	ARI	ARI	ARI	ARI	ARI	ARI	ARI	ARI	ARI	ARI	ARI	ARI	ARI	ARI	ARI	ARI
NE	NE	NE	NE	NE	NE	NE	NE	NE	NE	NE	NE	NE	NE	NE	NE	NE
MIA	MIA	MIA	MIA	MIA	MIA	MIA	MIA	MIA	MIA	MIA	MIA	MIA	MIA	MIA	MIA	MIA
BUF	BUF	BUF	BUF	BUF	BUF	BUF	BUF	BUF	BUF	BUF	BUF	BUF	BUF	BUF	BUF	BUF
NYJ	NYJ	NYJ	NYJ	NYJ	NYJ	NYJ	NYJ	NYJ	NYJ	NYJ	NYJ	NYJ	NYJ	NYJ	NYJ	NYJ
CIN	CIN	CIN	CIN	CIN	CIN	CIN	CIN	CIN	CIN	CIN	CIN	CIN	CIN	CIN	CIN	CIN
PIT	PIT	PIT	PIT	PIT	PIT	PIT	PIT	PIT	PIT	PIT	PIT	PIT	PIT	PIT	PIT	PIT
CLE	CLE	CLE	CLE	CLE	CLE	CLE	CLE	CLE	CLE	CLE	CLE	CLE	CLE	CLE	CLE	CLE
BAL	BAL	BAL	BAL	BAL	BAL	BAL	BAL	BAL	BAL	BAL	BAL	BAL	BAL	BAL	BAL	BAL
HOU	HOU	HOU	HOU	HOU	HOU	HOU	HOU	HOU	HOU	HOU	HOU	HOU	HOU	HOU	HOU	HOU
IND	IND	IND	IND	IND	IND	IND	IND	IND	IND	IND	IND	IND	IND	IND	IND	IND
TEN	TEN	TEN	TEN	TEN	TEN	TEN	TEN	TEN	TEN	TEN	TEN	TEN	TEN	TEN	TEN	TEN
JAX	JAX	JAX	JAX	JAX	JAX	JAX	JAX	JAX	JAX	JAX	JAX	JAX	JAX	JAX	JAX	JAX
DEN	DEN	DEN	DEN	DEN	DEN	DEN	DEN	DEN	DEN	DEN	DEN	DEN	DEN	DEN	DEN	DEN
KC	KC	KC	KC	KC	KC	KC	KC	KC	KC	KC	KC	KC	KC	KC	KC	KC
SD	SD	SD	SD	SD	SD	SD	SD	SD	SD	SD	SD	SD	SD	SD	SD	SD
OAK	OAK	OAK	OAK	OAK	OAK	OAK	OAK	OAK	OAK	OAK	OAK	OAK	OAK	OAK	OAK	OAK

GROCERY LIST FOR THIS WEEK
in case you need a cover for why you're watching football again.

GROCERY LIST FOR THIS WEEK
in case you need a cover for why you're watching football again.

SUPER BOWL 50 PREDICTIONS FROM KICKSTARTER SUPPORTERS

—

Jon Acuff	**Patriots** over Anyone
Richard Allain	**Packers** over Colts
Matt Bassuk	**Cowboys** over Broncos
Peter Carosa	**Bills** over Packers
Stew Conkle	**Packers** over Colts
Tor Constantino	**Bills** over Packers
Tripp Crosby	**Patriots** over Orioles
Nate DaCosta	**Patriots** over Packers
Mike Deraco	**Steelers** over Packers
Luke Dooley	**Bengals** over Eagles
Brian Donaldson	**Patriots** over Packers
Shawn Erb	**Packers** over Steelers
Callie Ferguson	**Packers** over Colts
Chad Gibbs	**Panthers** over Colts
Austin Gilly	**Broncos** over Cowboys
Jeff Goodrich	**Packers** over Patriots
Matt Gronseth	**Broncos** over Packers
Jon Hilton	**Eagles** over Steelers
Melinda Kaufman	**Eagles** over Patriots
Ron Millward	**Buffaloes** over Patriots
Aaron Motta	**Patriots** over Packers
Tom Motta	**Patriots** over Packers
Ernie Reppe	**Seahawks** over Steelers
Kevin Southam	**Dolphins** over Giants
Tyler Stanton	**Cowboys** over Patriots
Phil Stasyszen	**Packers** over Ravens
Jon Trippett	**Colts** over Packers
Michael Stoltzfus	**Packers** over Colts
Michael Wagner	**Packers** over Colts

PART V*
THE END

*The fifth part**

(it comes after part IV)*

***4 8 15 16 23 42.

THANK YOU

To Erica, Kylie, and Parker, thanks for letting me watch twenty-two guys in tight pants run around on grass as much as I do. I love you guys way more than I love football...it's not even close, really.

To Chris Dearolf and Jeff Goodrich, thanks for your help with the Kickstarter video, it was a huge factor in helping me hit my goal!

To Josh, thanks for encouraging me to stick with this project!

To my backers - the family, friends, and strangers - who made this book possible by supporting the Kickstarter campaign. Thank you all so much!

KICKSTARTER BACKERS: Tor Constantino, Kyle Reed, Shawn Smucker, Jeff Goodrich, Tim Payne, Chad Gibbs, Aaron Motta, Tyler Stanton, Jason Gausta, Mike Lukaszewski, Brian Hawn, Jon Acuff, Austin Gilly, Ernie Reppe, Alyssa Kawata, Tripp Crosby, Dan Geesaman, Erica Allain, David Henderson, Howard Fryberger, Mike Yoder, Peter Pollock, Justin Lemiuex, Peter Carosa, Phil Stasyszen, Nate & Kandace DaCosta, Rob Stennett, Bill Schultz, Richard Allain, Chris Dearolf, Dan Baudin, Dan West, Tom & Deb Motta, Steph Kandray, Gary Fisher, Ron Millward, Karyn Eaton, Matt Gronseth, Clay Morgan, Billy T, Jon Hilton, Neil Calfman, Callie Ferguson, Josh Allain, Kevin Haggerty, Jordan Allain, Doug & Melinda Kaufman, Sara Corman, Brian Donaldson, Hannah Rush, Keith Cotton, Al Segro, Joe Craven, Mike Stoltzfus, Tim Cranmer, Dave Pointek, Matt Sorenson, Donnie Murdock, Stewart Conkle, Phil Morris, Doris Hilton, Jon Graham, John Moulton, Jack Goodwin, Manny Olawale, Mike Vardy, Chad Jones, David Urrutia, Philip Wiebe, Michael Wagner, Meghan Hansen, Scott McClellan, Stephanie Stoller, Shawn Erb, Mike Deraco, David Barker, Jon Fisher, James O'Beirne, Craig Scott, Luke Dooley, Kevin Southam, Jeremy Motta, Jeff Holland, Caleb Stevenson, Matthew Paul Turner, Eman Stoltzfus, Ty Stoltzfus, Matt Bassuk, Dan Madigan, Annie Downs, Kyle Stanton, Radu Timbuc, Jeremy McKinney, Val Englerth, Eric Perry, Robert Keylor, Jeremy Casella, Denim Kurtzhals, Steve Goble, Nathan Smith, Sunny Siddhu, Jason Stoltzfus, Jesse Anderson, and Trina Lee.

FOR MORE

For more of this type of football nonsense, find yourself a computer or mobile device and check out my free football newsletter, The Slant, at ProFootballBeast.com/TheSlant/

For less, travel back in time to before you bought this book.

Made in the USA
Lexington, KY
10 October 2015